The Voice of the Bridegroom

The Voice of the Bridegroom

Preaching as an Expression of Spousal Love

BENJAMIN A. ROBERTS

WIPF & STOCK · Eugene, Oregon

THE VOICE OF THE BRIDEGROOM
Preaching as an Expression of Spousal Love

Copyright © 2021 Benjamin A. Roberts. All rights reserved. Except for brief quotations in critical publications or reviews, no part of this book may be reproduced in any manner without prior written permission from the publisher. Write: Permissions, Wipf and Stock Publishers, 199 W. 8th Ave., Suite 3, Eugene, OR 97401.

Scripture texts in this work are taken from the *New American Bible with Revised New Testament and Revised Psalms* © 1991, 1986, 1970 Confraternity of Christian Doctrine, Washington, D.C. and are used by permission of the copyright owner. All Rights Reserved. No part of the *New American Bible* may be reproduced in any form without permission in writing from the copyright owner.

Table 3.4 © Ken Hyland, 2018, *Metadiscourse: Exploring Interactions in Writing*, Continuum Publishing, used by permission of Bloomsbury Publishing Plc.

The English translation of Non-Biblical Readings from *The Liturgy of the Hours* © 1973, 1974, 1975, International Commission on English in the Liturgy Corporation (ICEL); excerpts from the English translation of *The Roman Missal* © 2010, ICEL. All rights reserved.

Wipf & Stock
An Imprint of Wipf and Stock Publishers
199 W. 8th Ave., Suite 3
Eugene, OR 97401

www.wipfandstock.com

PAPERBACK ISBN: 978-1-7252-9073-0
HARDCOVER ISBN: 978-1-7252-9074-7
EBOOK ISBN: 978-1-7252-9075-4

01/11/21

For all who preach in love to me
And
For all who hear me preach in love

With such affection for you, we were determined to share with you not only the gospel of God, but our very selves as well, so dearly beloved had you become to us.

—1 Thess 2:8

Contents

List of Tables	ix
Acknowledgments	xi
Introduction	xiii
Chapter 1 The Spousal Relationship: Husband and Wife	1
Chapter 2 The Spousal Relationship: Priest and Church	25
Chapter 3 Preaching: An Expression of Spousal Love	48
Strategy for Preparation in the Nuptial Hermeneutic	87
Homily Evaluation Rubric Survey	89
Two Sample Homilies	91
Bibliography	95

List of Tables

3.1	Symbols for Congregational Exegesis	56
3.2	Interpretive Principles	64
3.3	Metadiscourse	78

Acknowledgments

Learning is a relational act; there is no true learning outside of a relationship. I wish to thank my parents, my sister, Erin, and many friends and colleagues for encouraging me to pursue the degree which led to this book.

I thank the members of Aquinas Institute of Theology DMin Cohort 2014 for their support, humor, and friendship during our studies together. Additionally, I offer abundant gratitude to Honora Werner, OP; Gregory Heille, OP; and all of the Aquinas Institute faculty for their creativity and patience. In a very profound way, I offer thanks to my adviser, Jay Harrington, OP, and the Rev. Robert Pesarchick, STD, my reader, whose comments, counsel, and correction brought this project to completion.

I wish to express my appreciation to Dr. Carmina Chapp of Saint Joseph's College of Maine, as well as Dr. Steven Hyland and Dr. Jacob Wobig of Wingate University for working with me on elective courses and beyond. I also wish to thank my colleagues in the Catholic Association of Teachers of Homiletics and the Academy of Homiletics, especially Dr. Susan McGurgan and the Rev. Dr. Richard Eslinger, for their support, welcome, kindness and comments.

With a gratitude for which words are insufficient, I thank Lynn Drolet, the first-grade teacher who taught me, as a doctoral student, how to write the English language.

Finally, I thank the people of Our Lady of Lourdes Parish in Monroe, North Carolina. They received me as their own, supported me with their prayers, and enabled my growth as a preacher and a pastor. Echoing Saint Paul, I have the honor to share with them not only the gospel, but my very life, so dear they have become to me.

Introduction

PREACHING IS A RELATIONAL act. We preach in the context of a relationship. Martin Buber, in his classic work *I and Thou*, proposes two basic kinds of relationships: the I-It and the I-Thou.[1] An I-It relationship is "a one-sided experience of knowing, using and categorizing people and things."[2] On the other hand, I-Thou relationships are "direct, open, mutual, and present."[3] Foundational for this book is the notion that the relationship between the preacher and the assembly (that is, the community of hearers) is an I-Thou relationship.

There are multiple types of I-Thou relationships and several of them could be used to describe the relationship between the preacher and the assembly. First, in the Christian context, the preacher is a fellow believer with the members of the assembly; together, they are all disciples of Jesus Christ. United as followers of the Lord, the preacher offers testimony to the power of the Gospel. Second, the preacher is a teacher of the faith. The preacher catechizes the members of the assembly. Third, the preacher, as pastor, is the shepherd of the flock. In this relationship, the preacher guides, exhorts, admonishes, and encourages the members of the assembly through preaching. This book proposes another dimension to the I-Thou relationship between the preacher and the assembly: bridegroom and bride, the spousal dimension.

---

1. Martin Buber, *I and Thou*, 53.
2. Kramer and Gawlick, *Martin Buber's I and Thou*, 42.
3. Kramer and Gawlick, *Martin Buber's I and Thou*, 42.

In this book, the image of bridegroom and bride, a spousal relationship, will be explored as a metaphor for the relationship between the preacher and the assembly. Following this exploration, preaching will be proposed and examined as an expression of spousal love. Prior to describing the outline of this book, it is important to recount the origin of this project.

ORIGIN AND INTENT OF THE BOOK

This book began as part of my doctoral work and was born from a personal crisis and renewal. As I approached the sixth anniversary of priestly ordination in 2015, I experienced a significant loss in my enthusiasm for ministry in general and more specifically preaching. The fire that had once burned brightly was now reduced to a few smoldering coals providing scant heat and very limited light. During the annual priests' retreat for the diocese, I discussed this experience with approximately fifteen other priests. Those ordained less than five years could not relate. Every priest ordained more than ten years easily remembered their own personal experience with this phenomenon. All of them said that they faced a similar crisis in their second five years of ministry. Most of them said that the seventh year was one of the most difficult of their ministry. Shortly after the retreat, I discussed this lack of enthusiasm and the timeline mentioned by those experienced priests with a few married couples. All of them responded, "Seven years, it is just like marriage!"

The notion of the "seven-year itch" in marriage is deeply embedded in popular imagination. Additionally, there is some scientific basis for this timely struggle. In one study, Dr. Larry A. Kurdek, late professor of psychology at Wright State University in Dayton, OH, found a steep decline in marital satisfaction at both the fourth year and the seventh year of marriage.[4] A study conducted by the University of Michigan utilized the seventh and sixteenth years of marriage to analyze boredom and marital quality.[5] The US Census Bureau found that, on average, those couples who divorced had separated after seven years and divorced the following year.[6]

A similar phenomenon to the seven-year marital experience seems to exist among preachers and priests. Karl Barth, while not giving a specific year, briefly notes the desert experience for the preacher which occurs after a few years of ministry. He writes that "a time of drought and emptiness will set in which only too easily can discourage and frustrate them," in which

---

4. Berger, "Study Finds a 7-Year Itch, and a 4-Year One," para. 14.
5. University of Michigan, "Seven-year Itch? Boredom Can Hurt A Marriage," para. 4.
6. Roberts, "Majority of Marriages End Before 25 Years, Census Finds," para. 8.

"they disconsolately scrape together the few things they still have left to say and realize that sooner or later these fruitful oases will disappear and give way to unrelenting desert."[7] In one of the studies by Dean R. Hoge, the seventh year after ordination was the average year when priests who chose to resign left active ministry.[8] The seventh year and the years that surround it are a time ripe for a renewing intervention.

The proclamation of the gospel, particularly in the celebration of the liturgy, is at the heart of priestly ministry.[9] Preaching is fundamental; it is a constitutive part of priestly identity. Therefore, a renewal of preaching can begin with a renewed understanding of identity. As noted earlier, preaching is a relational act in which the priest preaches as a fellow disciple, a teacher of the faith, a shepherd of the flock, and as a bridegroom to the bride. The notion of the priest as bridegroom or spouse was promoted by Pope Saint John Paul II in the 1992 Apostolic Exhortation *Pastores Dabo Vobis*. He writes, "The priest is called to be the living image of Jesus Christ, the spouse of the Church," and "In his spiritual life, therefore, he is called to live out Christ's spousal love toward the Church, his bride."[10] The notion of the spousal relationship between the priest and the church was also included in the Congregation for the Clergy's 1994 *Directory on the Life and Ministry of Priests*.[11] Since then, other contemporary theologians including Cardinal Angelo Scola, Cardinal Marc Ouellette, Bishop Andrew Cozzens, and Sr. Sara Butler, MSBT, have expounded on this spousal relationship.[12] Exploring the spousal relationship between the priest and the church and applying that relationship to the ministry of preaching offers an additional model for priests in their ministry and preaching.

Seeking to contribute an additional model for preaching, principally for priests, my intent in this book is to present a nuptial vision of the preaching ministry. In so doing, I hope to offer a renewed approach that may assist priests who experience a lack of enthusiasm or even burnout after several

7. Barth, *Homiletics*, 91–92.

8. Hoge, *Experiences of Priests Ordained Five to Nine Years*, 174–75.

9. Vatican Council II, *Presbyterorum Ordinis*. 4. See Wallace, *Preaching in the Sunday Assembly*, 59–60.

10. John Paul II, *Pastores Dabo Vobis*, 22.

11. Congregation for the Clergy. *Directory on the Ministry and Life of* Priests, 13. On February 11, 2013, the Congregation for the Clergy issued a new edition of the *Directory*. However, it was not widely published, is not available from the United States Conference of Catholic Bishops, and as of October 2020, there is no English translation of this work on the website of the Congregation for the Clergy. For these reasons, all references in this work are to the 1994 edition of the *Directory*.

12. See Scola, *Nuptial Mystery*; Ouellet, *Mystery and Sacrament of Love*; Cozzens, "*Imago Vivens Iesu Christi Sponsi Ecclesiae*"; Butler, *Catholic Priesthood and Women*.

years in ministry. When we are able to renew our relationship with preaching through our relationship with God's people, we stir into flame the gift that is within us.

Additionally, this book can be of use to seminarians. When I was in my third year of theological studies, I took courses in the theology of marriage and the theology of the priesthood in the fall semester. In the spring semester, I took a course in the theology of preaching. This book would have been extremely helpful during both semesters. As noted in the outline of this book which follows in the next section, this work summarizes and explores both the theology of marriage and the theology of the priesthood before moving into a theological and practical exploration of preaching.

OUTLINE OF THE BOOK

The plan for this book, along with a brief description of the chapters, is presented in this section. In addition to this introduction and appendices, there are three chapters in this book. However, before outlining the chapters, it is important to introduce a new descriptive term which was developed by me and is utilized in this writing.

During the early stages of research into the relationship between husband and wife, I developed a new descriptive term for the spousal relationship: *mutual kenotic vulnerability*. This term indicates that the relationship is constituted by the consent of each of the parties, involves self-emptying or a gift of self, and is open to the possibility of fruitfulness or harm for both parties. It is a relationship that is chosen or at least actively accepted. It involves personal sacrifice and a certain level of risk. Elizabeth O'Donnell Gandolfo notes, "Vulnerability not only exposes human beings to harm, it is also the condition for the possibility of healing, health, and wholeness."[13] In the chapters of the book, the descriptor *mutual kenotic vulnerability* will be applied to the spousal relationship between husband and wife, between the priest and the church, and to the relationship between the preacher and the assembly.[14] Having introduced the new descriptive term utilized in this book, the following describes the chapters of the project.

Chapter 1 presents an examination of the spousal relationship between husband and wife. Rooted in the nuptial vision of Pope St. John Paul II, this chapter explores anthropology, asymmetrical reciprocity, marital love, the

---

13. Gandolfo, *Power and Vulnerability of Love*, 3. For an additional perspective on vulnerability see Culp, *Vulnerability and Glory*.

14. The model for the preacher's kenotic action is the kenotic action of Jesus as expressed in Phil 2:5–8.

conjugal bond and good of the spouses, fruitfulness and responsible parenthood, and marital spirituality. The chapter concludes with an examination of Pope St. John Paul II's analysis of Ephesians 5:21–33.

Chapter 2 examines the spousal relationship between the priest and the church. It provides an overview of the ministerial priesthood, a brief biblical examination of Jesus as Bridegroom, the relationship between the royal and ministerial participations in the priesthood of Christ, charity, the sacramental character and bond, fruitfulness, and spirituality.

Chapter 3 proposes preaching as an expression of spousal love. The chapter examines nuptiality as a theological category and presents the seven characteristics of nuptial hermeneutic for preaching. These characteristics are utilized to explore the assembly, the preacher, the homily, and the homiletical method. The chapter concludes with a strategy for preaching using the nuptial hermeneutic.

In the appendix I have included a one-page summary of the strategy for preaching, a rubric for homily analysis which looks at the experience of the hearer, and two sample homilies.

While the preaching relationship is always in need of renewal, a single image or metaphor for the preaching act is insufficient for all preachers. This project explores the preaching relationship as a spousal relationship. The final section of this introduction notes the intended audience and recognizes some of the limitations of this nuptial vision of preaching.

AUDIENCE AND LIMITATIONS

The nuptial vision of preaching proposed in this book was constructed by a parish pastor and is intended principally for parish pastors. With this intention, I mean in no way to negate the important homiletical contributions that missionaries, weekend priest assistants, deacons, women and men religious, and lay preachers make to the preaching ministry of the church. The multiplicity of preachers and forms of preaching in the church are great graces for the works of evangelization, catechesis, and sanctification. As noted above, a single image or metaphor for preachers is not sufficient for the many manifestations of preaching. The nuptial metaphor, in my opinion, is particularly fitting for the parish pastor.[15] This work intends principally to assist parish pastors in their preaching ministry.

One of the chief characteristics of the office of pastor is stability. While this aspect of stability is often neglected, pastoral stability is normative in

15. The usefulness of the nuptial hermeneutic for preaching to preachers other than parish pastors is an important area for further study.

the law of the church. Canon 522 states, "A pastor must possess stability and therefore is to be appointed for an indefinite period of time. The diocesan bishop can appoint him only for a specific period if the conference of bishops has permitted this by a decree."[16] There are several authors in recent years who have reflected on the importance of pastoral stability. In a 2009 article, Fr. Mark A. Pilon noted the importance of stability for the pastor in terms of his relationship to the bishop, the parish, and the priest's own sense of identity and ministry. He writes, "When such changes take place every five or six years, or even every ten years, it should not surprise us if some, perhaps many, pastors suffer from the lack of stability in their personal lives and their role as pastor."[17] Noting the effect of frequent or regular transfers of pastors on parishioners, Pilon continues, "Likewise, it should not surprise us that many parishioners no longer feel confident to entrust their personal and spiritual needs to such a transient spiritual guide."[18] Echoing these sentiments in a 2013 article, George Weigel proposed pastoral stability as an essential component for the success of the New Evangelization.[19] In a 2018 work, Gwendolen Adams posits that pastoral stability supports the work of evangelization and vocations. She concludes that the stability of the pastor "can cultivate prayerfully discerned vocations, raising up the priests, religious, and married couples who are the indispensable witnesses of Christ and his Church, and it facilitates those apostolic works by which witnesses bring the loving personal experience of Christ to people who do not know him."[20] While these authors do not specifically address the impact of pastoral stability on preaching, they do address the importance of stability for the overall ministry of the parish. As will be explored later in this work, a stable pastoral relationship in which the preacher and the community are able to grow and mature together, is one of the central characteristics of the nuptial vision for preaching. For this reason, the nuptial hermeneutic for preaching is particularly fitting for parish pastors. At the same time, the characteristic of a stable pastoral relationship is one of the principal limitations of this vision of preaching.

---

16. *Code of Canon Law*, 522.
17. Pilon, "Pastors and Stability of Office," para. 11.
18. Pilon, "Pastors and Stability of Office," para. 11.
19. Weigel, "Pastors Are Not Interchangeable Parts."
20. Adams, "Importance of Geographic Stability for the Church," para. 18.

CONCLUSION

This introduction presented the origin and need of this project and its twofold intention, introduced the new descriptive term *mutual kenotic vulnerability*, described the chapters, noted the intended audience, and recognized some of the limitations of the project. Having reviewed these foundational elements, the first step in creating the nuptial hermeneutic begins with the exploration of the spousal relationship between husband and wife.

Chapter 1

The Spousal Relationship

Husband and Wife

THE SPOUSAL RELATIONSHIP BETWEEN a husband and wife is a multi-faceted reality. While not intending to present a complete theology of marriage, this chapter examines selected aspects of the spousal relationship.[1] These aspects include the anthropological considerations of complementarity and asymmetrical reciprocity of human persons, the nature of marital love, the conjugal bond and the good of the spouses, fruitfulness and responsible parenthood, and marital spirituality. This chapter concludes with an examination of the nuptial vision of Pope Saint John Paul II presented in his analysis of Ephesians 5 and a description of marriage as a relationship of *mutual kenotic vulnerability*.[2]

---

1. For a more complete theological and historical examination of marriage and family, see Cahall, *Mystery of Marriage*; Rubio, *Christian Theology of Marriage and Family*; and Ouellet, *Mystery and Sacrament of Love*.

2. *Mutual kenotic vulnerability*, as described in the Introduction, indicates that the relationship is constituted by the consent of both parties, involves self-emptying or a gift of self, and is open to the possibility of fruitfulness or harm for both parties.

AN ADEQUATE ANTHROPOLOGY

The first aspect of the spousal relationship is a correct understanding of the human person. An analysis of the specific communion of persons that is marriage begins with an anthropological evaluation. The Enlightenment division of the inseparable connection between soul and body, and the subsequent devaluation of the body, received both a philosophical and theological challenge from the teachings of Pope Saint John Paul II, specifically in his Wednesday audiences from September, 1979 through November, 1984. He sought to reestablish the biblical notion of the unity of the human person.[3] Appealing to the beginning of creation and the original state of the human person as created by God, he proposes four constitutive facets of the human person. Before the entry of sin into the world, man experienced original solitude, original unity, original nakedness, and original innocence.[4] These are critical concepts which provide the foundation for the examination of marriage.

Original solitude is the first constitutive facet of the human person according to Pope Saint John Paul II.[5] Original solitude concerns the relationship between the human person and every other creature. The human person is unique; only the human person recognizes himself as an individual. As presented in the second creation story of Genesis (Gen 2:4–25) in which the male and female are created separately, all of the creatures of the world are recognized as something different from the man. Only with the creation of the female does the male recognize a creature like himself. The male achieves understanding of himself only when he encounters the female. The original solitude is complemented by the second facet of the human person, original unity, in which human nature is created and expressed as male or female.[6] The complete expression of human nature is seen in the female and the male, and they are created for each other. Together they constitute the image of God.[7] They form a communion of persons, capable of self-gift to each other through a reciprocal choice and expressed definitively in one flesh union. Pope Saint John Paul II offers the notion of original nakedness, the third facet of the human person, as part of the relationship between the male and female prior to sin and shame. This is a recognition of the goodness and giftedness of the other, particularly the body of the

---

3. For further discussion and background see Bransfield, *Human Person*, 73–117.
4. John Paul II, *Theology of the Body*, 146–204.
5. John Paul II, *Theology of the Body*, 146–56.
6. John Paul II, *Theology of the Body*, 156–59.
7. John Paul II, *Theology of the Body*, 163.

other. It is also an affirmation of the goodness of the body itself. There is no objectification of the other or of oneself in original nakedness.[8] The fourth facet of the human person is original innocence, which is essentially a state of consciousness. It means that the male and the female recognize their own dignity, the dignity of the other, the meaning of their bodies and capacity for gift, and uninhibited communion with God.[9] These four concepts serve as pillars upon which an adequate anthropology is built.

The Three Meanings of the Body

At the heart of his anthropological vision, Pope Saint John Paul II presents three meanings of the body: filial, spousal, and parental.[10] The spousal meaning of the body is central to his presentation with the filial meaning, which is foundational, and the parental meaning, which is consequential. Built upon the filial, the spousal meaning flows into the parental. Each of the three meanings is rooted in the concept of gift.

The filial meaning of the body is creation itself. The human person is created in the image and likeness of God and experiences creation through the body. Conscious of personhood, he or she recognizes that the gift of being comes from another. This is the first and fundamental relationship. In the filial meaning of the body, the person recognizes his or her body, spirit, and personhood as a gift *from* another.[11]

The spousal or nuptial meaning of the body is presented in the creation of the human person as male or female. The human person is created for relationship. The pope describes this spousal meaning as "the power to express love: precisely that love in which the human person becomes a gift—and through this gift—fulfills the very meaning of his being and existence."[12] With the filial meaning, the human person is a gift *from* God. In the spousal meaning, the human person is a gift *for* the other. The recognition of creation from gift and for gift "constitutes the fundamental component of human existence in the world."[13]

The third meaning of the body is the parental meaning. The spousal meaning of the body, realized in the one-flesh union between the male and

---

8. John Paul II, *Theology of the Body*, 169–78.
9. John Paul II, *Theology of the Body*, 191–204.
10. John Paul II, *Theology of the Body*, 178–91. See also Anderson and Granados, *Called to Love*, 168–69.
11. John Paul II, *Theology of the Body*, 178–82.
12. John Paul II, *Theology of the Body*, 185–86.
13. John Paul II, *Theology of the Body*, 189.

the female, is fecund. The complementarity of the male and the female, which is both physical and metaphysical, is placed at the service of fruitfulness in such a way that in giving themselves as a gift to each other they cooperate with God in the blessing of new life. Through the spouses' mutual self-gift, God gives the gift of filiation again. This is a manifestation of overflowing communion and cooperation between God and the spouses. The parental meaning bears the character of a gift as a result of the proper fulfillment of the spousal meaning of the body.[14] The parental meaning, at least in its physical sense, is not merely the product of human action.

These three meanings of the body, filial, spousal, and parental, present a trinity of relationships which are inscribed in the nature of every human person. These relationships build one upon the other in the development of the individual human person and the communion of persons that is the spousal relationship.

Asymmetrical Reciprocity

Building on the work of Pope Saint John Paul II, Angelo Scola presents a further anthropological insight in his examination of the spousal relationship. He notes that sexual difference, as an aspect of the nuptial mystery, is of critical importance. It is the anthropological starting point for human relationship and is irreducible.[15] Scola notes that sexual difference is something beyond simple complementarity. A plurality of human relationship is possible because of complementarity. These relationships would include paternity and maternity, sorority and fraternity, and friendship.[16] As it applies to nuptiality, sexual difference reflects an asymmetrical reciprocity. The human person, as male or female, is placed from the very beginning in relationship to the other. The two expressions of human personhood, male and female, are ordered to each other. Asymmetrical reciprocity enables the unity of the two, even as each maintains their individuality. Asymmetrical reciprocity facilitates a dual unity. The individuals are not absorbed into each other or annihilated; they do not form some androgynous union of two halves. The dual unity of the two is ordered to the procreation of another. Asymmetrical reciprocity is the necessary condition for nuptiality.[17]

---

14. John Paul II, *Theology of the Body*, 196–98.
15. Scola, *The Nuptial Mystery*, 92–96.
16. Scola, *The Nuptial Mystery*, 119.
17. Scola, *The Nuptial Mystery*, 95.

Summary of Anthropological Evaluation

This brief anthropological evaluation flowing from the teachings of Pope St. John Paul II proposes a vision of the human person which is existential, embodied, and relational. The human person is created with the capacity for self-knowledge, self-gift, and personal growth. A person is embodied, either as male or female, and created for relationship with the other. This asymmetrical and reciprocal relationship is the necessary condition for fruitfulness. The human person was not created for isolation but to be part of a communion. The anthropological foundation which views the human person as created from gift and for gift finds both its motivation and expression in love.

MARITAL LOVE

The second aspect of the spousal relationship is the nature of marital love. The joy of love is at the center of the spousal relationship. Love provides the motivation for the entering into and remaining in the spousal relationship. Spousal love is an activity of the whole person and not simply an expression of the emotions. Various theologians in the past century have explored the nature of this love; this section provides a brief analysis of some of those contributions.

Dietrich Von Hildebrand

Reflection on the theology of marriage was swept into the philosophical current of personalism with Dietrich Von Hildebrand's work *Marriage: The Mystery of Faithful Love*. Published in German in 1929 and widely translated in the succeeding years, this brief work anticipates and foreshadows the theological and pastoral reflection on marriage of the decades that followed. He presents a vision of marriage rooted in the notion of a natural institution, although of divine origin, which is then elevated to sacramental dignity.[18] In his analysis he offers a careful distinction between conjugal love and marriage. Conjugal love is a unique kind of relationship. It is an activity of the whole person: it involves the mutual giving of one's self, is made possible because of sexual difference and complementarity, and moves the partners to live both with and for the beloved. As a complete gift of self,

---

18. Hildebrand, *Marriage*, 3. For a brief overview of philosophical personalism see Burke, *Man and Values*, 186–93.

conjugal love is exclusive.[19] Marriage, however, is constituted by a formal act of the will expressed in some solemn way and is fully actualized in sexual consummation. These actions bring the marriage into being and "it persists as such, regardless of the sentiments or attitudes of the partners."[20] This is a critical difference between conjugal love and marriage. A person can fall in love. He or she cannot fall into marriage. Discussing the nature of love within the context of marriage, Hildebrand notes that this love must be willed, protected, cherished, and nurtured. It must be protected from distractions and temptations as well as the competition from other lesser goods. Love is a task given to each of the spouses to both offer to and accept from the other.[21] Von Hildebrand's implications for this marital love were furthered by Pope Saint Paul VI.

Pope Saint Paul VI

Nearly forty years after the publication of Dietrich Von Hildebrand's insightful book on marriage, Pope Saint Paul VI issued his final encyclical, *Humanae Vitae*, in 1968. In this encyclical, the Pope enumerates four characteristics of love in marriage. The first characteristic is that marital love is human; it is an activity of the whole person and a deliberate choice. In marriage, the spouses join together in the closest of intimacy, both spiritual and physical, and through this relationship grow toward human fulfillment. A second characteristic is that this love is total. The Pope mentions marriage as a particular kind of friendship involving mutual sharing and an altruistic love between the spouses. Faithfulness and exclusivity until death is the third characteristic. Finally, marital love is fecund: it possesses a fruitfulness that is both physical and spiritual.[22] The fruitfulness of marital love will be discussed in a later section of this chapter.

Angelo Scola

Angelo Cardinal Scola offers a third perspective on the nature of spousal love. Scola, who provides the notion of asymmetrical reciprocity, envisions love as the second aspect of the nuptial mystery. In his tripartite schema, love bridges the foundational aspect which is the asymmetrical reciprocity

---

19. Hildebrand, *Marriage*, 7–21.
20. Hildebrand, *Marriage*, 22.
21. Hildebrand, *Marriage*, 32–35.
22. Paul VI, *Humanae Vitae*, 9.

of sexual difference and the third aspect of the mystery which is fruitfulness.[23] As asymmetrical reciprocity provides the condition for nuptiality, love provides the motivation. Love possesses the capacity to unify the other two components of nuptiality. Scola notes two different aspects of love: love as a need and love as a gift. The concept of love as a need responds to the human experience of limitation or lack. This existential and personal experience of lack calls the person outside of themselves. Within the experience of love as a need resides the invitation to offer love as a gift. Authentic love progresses from the desire for reception to a willingness for oblation. Love as gift springs from the ground of love as lack; that is, an insufficiency or incompleteness. It is important to note that the experience of love as limit or lack is not necessarily egotistical love of self, though it can be corrupted into such. Whenever love as lack or limit seeks fulfillment by denying the oblative dimension, that is the procreative power, then the potential gift of self descends into selfishness. Love is the motivation which fuels the engine of nuptiality made possible by sexual difference and fulfilled in procreation.[24]

Pope Francis

Subsequent to the works of Angelo Cardinal Scola and Pope Saint Paul VI and nearly a century after the work of Dietrich Von Hildebrand, Pope Francis offers an analysis of love in the spousal relationship. Pope Francis presents a profound pastoral meditation on love in the marital relationship in his Apostolic Exhortation *Amoris Laetitia*.[25] Placed at the center of this lengthy document, the Holy Father examines the hymn of love from the thirteenth chapter of the First Letter to the Corinthians. He moves from a linguistic analysis and commentary on each of the attributes of love to a discussion of some key aspects of conjugal love. The discussion of love proffered in this Pauline passage contains descriptions of what love is, of what love is not, and of the functional capacities of love.

Beginning with what love is, Paul states that love is patient, kind, and generous. Commenting on patience, Pope Francis explains this attribute as meaning that love is not impulsive or offensive. It allows time for conversion and reconciliation. Patience is a necessary condition for the sharing of mercy. Kindness concerns external behavior: it is inner goodness manifested in action. Kindness indicates a love that is ever ready to assist, to offer

---

23. Scola, *Nuptial Mystery*, 122.
24. Scola, *Nuptial Mystery*, 122.
25. Francis, *Amoris Laetitia*, chapter 4, 89–154.

service, and to provide for the benefit of the other.[26] Generosity describes love as unselfish giving. This is sacrificial love which does not seek the benefit of the lover, but only the fulfillment of the beloved. This is the facet of love which motivates the laying down of one's life.[27] These positive aspects of love provide an internal disposition in patience, an external behavior in kindness, and a sacrificial dimension in generosity.

Traveling along the *via negativa*, what love is not, Paul notes that love is not jealous, not boastful, not rude, and not irritable or resentful. Jealousy would allow the lover to be saddened or discomforted by the success of the beloved. This internal disposition would restrict happiness. If love were boastful, then a spirit of unhealthy competition and a desire for superiority and domination can enter the relationship. This external behavior demeans the beloved. Pope Francis, offering a very concrete example, particularly cautions against a Christian boasting about knowledge of the faith to those who are not as well catechized.[28] Rudeness, in the thinking of the Holy Father, indicates an attitude that inflicts suffering on others. It is the opposite of gentleness and inhibits encounter. Rudeness is behavior, specifically speech, against the beloved. Pope Francis concludes the journey along the way of negation by stating that love is not irritable or resentful. This deeply internal disposition expects perfection from others and leads to isolation for the individual. It reflects a hardened heart. These characteristics are presented in the negative because jealousy, boastfulness, rudeness, irritability and resentment exclude love.[29]

The final element of this scriptural analysis reveals the actions which flow from love. The conclusion of this examination of 1 Corinthians 13:4–7 presents some of love's functional capacities. Love forgives, rejoices with others, bears all things, believes all things, hopes all things, and endures all things.[30] The ability to forgive is rooted in a prior experience of forgiveness. One is better able to forgive having first experienced the forgiveness of God. Forgiveness is the opposite of resentment; it seeks understanding and not isolation.[31] Rejoicing with others excludes a spirit of competition. Bearing all things allows for a relationship between two imperfect persons; it also concerns speech, according to Pope Francis. Love that believes all things denotes a relationship of trust and allows a sense of personal freedom which

---

26. Francis, *Amoris Laetitia*, 91–94.
27. Francis, *Amoris Laetitia*, 101–2. Cf. John 15:13.
28. Francis, *Amoris Laetitia*, 98.
29. Francis, *Amoris Laetitia*, 95–104.
30. Francis, *Amoris Laetitia*, 105–19.
31. Francis, *Amoris Laetitia*, 105–8.

enables personal growth. The notion of love that hopes all things regards the ability to see potential. The hope expressed here is that which desires the full flowering of the spouse. The final functional capacity is that love endures all things. This means that love is ready to meet any challenge and is unwilling to surrender.[32] The aspects of forgiveness, rejoicing, bearing, believing, hoping, and enduring are essential for continuation of the relationship.

Following the scriptural analysis, Pope Francis turns to pastoral counsel. These sections of chapter 4 of *Amoris Laetitia* are theologically rooted and very practical in approach.[33] The advice provided in these passages reveals a lifetime of ministerial experience with married couples. The Holy Father utilizes the categories of growth, passion, and transformation for married couples in this examination.

In the section on growth in conjugal love, Pope Francis recalls that marriage is a reflection of the covenant between God and humanity. Furthermore, marriage is an icon of the love of God for his people and renders visible the love of Christ for the church. The Pope is careful to note that while the divine relationship is perfect, the human relationship of marriage exists between two imperfect people.[34] In the communion of the imperfect, a lifelong commitment is only possible with a greater vision than what is immediate and with the aid of divine grace. Marriage is more than consent or a contract; it is an expression of a mature and loving decision to embrace the other. The Pope reaffirms that the commitment of marriage is faithful, indissoluble, and open to new life.

In this same section on growth, Pope Francis comments on the importance of joy and beauty in the spousal relationship.[35] Joy is cultivated; beauty is contemplated. The joy that shares in the triumphs and sorrows of the spouses and the bond between them must receive attentive care. This care and concern flows from contemplating the beloved. The Pope invites the spouses to contemplate each other, to gaze at each other, and recognize the dignity and value of the other. He writes, "Love opens our eyes and enables us to see, beyond all else, the great worth of a human being."[36] Contemplation enables recognition. Recognition sustains joy. Joy overflows in action and speech. The overflowing joy is manifested in attentive and loving words in a context of dialogue. Pope Francis emphasizes the importance of words in the spousal relationship: "The right words, spoken at the right time, daily

32. Francis, *Amoris Laetitia*, 109–19.
33. Francis, *Amoris Laetitia*, 120–64.
34. Francis, *Amoris Laetitia*, 121–22.
35. Francis, *Amoris Laetitia*, 126–28.
36. Francis, *Amoris Laetitia*, 128.

protect and nurture love."[37] Love is sustained and amplified by careful and attentive speech; communication is at the heart of marital communion.

The second category of this pastoral counsel is passionate love.[38] Pope Francis offers a positive view of the passions. Every virtuous human act flows from a passion properly governed by reason. Passions are not to be neglected or rejected, though they must be submitted to the good. The Holy Father notes that "a love lacking in either pleasure or passion is insufficient to symbolize the union of the human heart with God."[39] If passion is an essential component of the divine and human relationship, then it is certainly an appropriate component of the relationship between two humans. Passion and emotion find their proper fulfillment when they motivate a gift of self and not a selfish act. Since this can be said of sexual desire, the Pope seeks to present, in a very brief form, a positive vision of sexuality. Sexual desire and erotic love are part of the goodness of love in the spousal relationship. This aspect is a gift from God and designed to be a gift to and from the spouses. Whenever sexuality is used as a form of entertainment, gratification, domination, or selfishness, then the gift is corrupted and abused. The gift of sexuality, properly reverenced and respected, is a source of blessing and grace for the spouses.[40]

The final category of marital love in this pastoral counsel is transformation. This signifies the effect of love on the spouses and on their relationship; it is a maturing of the commitment. Transformation occurs over time and results from the daily renewal of the spousal bond. As the years pass and the spouses change physically and emotionally, the bond of their love calls them to confirm again their lifelong and fruitful commitment. This is only possible with the daily attention of the spouses and the aid of divine grace.[41]

The multifaceted mystery of love expressed in the First Letter to the Corinthians finds a concrete expression in the spousal relationship. Through an examination of the text and explanation of concepts flowing from this passage, Pope Francis presents a vision of love in marriage that is biblical, theological, and pastoral. Bringing an additional perspective on marital love to the work of Dietrich Von Hildebrand, Pope Saint Paul VI, and Angelo Cardinal Scola, the insights of Pope Francis illuminate the scriptural texts with the light of pastoral experience for the good of the spouses.

---

37. Francis, *Amoris Laetitia*, 133.
38. Francis, *Amoris Laetitia*, 142–49.
39. Francis, *Amoris Laetitia*, 142.
40. Francis, *Amoris Laetitia*, 150–57.
41. Francis, *Amoris Laetitia*, 163–64.

Summary of Marital Love

While the anthropological evaluation provides the necessary conditions for the spousal relationship, love provides the motivation and the content. As an activity of the whole person and involving a permanent gift of self, conjugal love unites the spouses in a union which provides the setting for growth and development, fruitfulness, and sanctification. This relationship, however, requires the attention of both parties. In order for this love to endure, the spouses must protect, cherish and nurture it. These endurance-enhancing actions are accomplished through forgiveness, attentive communication, and passionate respect. The multidimensional love which the spouses share joins them in an enduring conjugal bond and provides the foundation for the good of the spouses.

THE CONJUGAL BOND AND THE GOOD OF THE SPOUSES

The third aspect of the spousal relationship explores the conjugal bond and the good of the spouses. The conjugal bond and the good of the spouses are intimately related concepts. The bond that arises from the mutual consent of the spouses and sexual consummation unites the spouses in a relationship which extends beyond themselves. The spouses share in a conjugal bond which is extrinsic to them and is, by its nature as an expression of a complete and irrevocable gift of self, indissoluble. While a natural marriage (that is, between two unbaptized persons) shares a conjugal bond, the characteristics of the conjugal bond of a sacramental marriage between a baptized woman and a baptized man is the focus of our examination.[42]

The Conjugal Bond

Dietrich Von Hildebrand, in his foundational work *Marriage: The Mystery of Faithful Love*, provides a careful analysis of the conjugal bond in a sacramental marriage. More than simply a natural marriage with an ecclesiastical blessing, a sacramental marriage is the natural institution transfigured into the supernatural order.[43] In a sacramental marriage, the identity of the spouses receives a dignity beyond husband and wife. Each of the spouses

---

42. For a discussion of the conjugal bond of natural marriage, see Fornés, "Commentary on Canon 1134," 1523–26.

43. Hildebrand, *Marriage*, 41.

is an image of God for the other, a fellow member of the mystical body of Christ.[44] The relationship is elevated in such a way that in loving each other, each spouse loves Christ.[45]

In a sacramental marriage, the ultimate goal of marriage changes. In a natural marriage, the temporal good, welfare, and development of the partner is at the center. A sacramental marriage has for its ultimate goal the desire for satisfaction and eternal life for the beloved.[46] The relationship is not simply a path to happiness and human development in this life, but a privileged path in which the Kingdom of God is experienced and realized in the lives of the spouses. The union of the couple is rooted in Christ and blessed by Christ. The spouses are companions for each other in their consecration to Christ. A sacramental marriage is not only the union of two: it is the union of two in the One. The marriage bond belongs to Christ. The spouses, consecrated by baptism and the marriage covenant to give themselves to Christ in each other, exist in a communion greater than themselves.

The sacred communion of a sacramental marriage is a form of divine service; it is an act of praise and thanksgiving. The spouses, who are the essential ministers of the sacrament of marriage, offer worship to God as they faithfully live in the communion of love established by mutual consent. Through this mutual consent, the spouses enter into a sacred bond which becomes for them a source of grace. The natural institution of marriage from the order of creation now participates in the order of grace. The further development of this bond is that the communion of love in the sacrament of marriage which is sacred becomes a community of love which sanctifies.[47] Not only is it holy, it possesses the power to make holy.

The sacred communion of a sacramental marriage is a form of divine witness: sacramental marriage is an image of Christ and the church.[48] A sacramental marriage has been inserted into this relationship and in this participation of the Christ-church union achieves the full development of the nuptial relationship. The indissolubility, which is part of the nature of marriage, is elevated in its sacramental form to a sign of Christ's indissoluble relationship with the church. This elevated relationship effects for the spouses a deeper union with Christ and it provides for the spouses a place for their own growth in virtue and holiness. The indissoluble nature of a sacramental marriage protects this specific communion of love as a place

---

44. Hildebrand, *Marriage*, 44.
45. Hildebrand, *Marriage*, 46.
46. Hildebrand, *Marriage*, 46.
47. Hildebrand, *Marriage*, 49–53.
48. Hildebrand, *Marriage*, 56–57.

of grace, mercy, holiness, and wisdom. Hildebrand notes that fulfilling this difficult task of love in marriage requires a heroic spirit of generosity and sacrifice.[49]

The bond of a sacramental marriage establishes a sanctifying community in Christ. The bond is a source of grace for the spouses and a source of blessing beyond the spouses. The couple, as a union in Christ, offers the divine service of worship and the divine witness of signifying the union of Christ and the Church. A sacramental marriage is a communion of persons which both glorifies and testifies. Within this sacred bond, the spouses participate in a relationship which leads to growth, development, and holiness in pursuit of the good of the spouses.

The Good of the Spouses

Directly related to the conjugal bond is the good of the spouses. The term *good of the spouses (bonum coniugum)* entered into the official vocabulary of the Catholic Church with the 1983 Code of Canon Law.[50] This is a category apart from the three goods of marriage proposed by Saint Augustine and the primary and secondary ends of marriage provided by Saint Thomas Aquinas. The concept of the good of the spouses is rooted in philosophical personalism and reflects the teaching of the Second Vatican Council and Pope Saint John Paul II. Cormac Burke offers a thorough analysis of this aspect of marriage.

Burke grounds his examination of the good of the spouses in the new definition of matrimonial consent presented in the 1983 Code.[51] The concept of the mutual giving and accepting of the spouses presented in this new definition reflects a considerable development from older definitions of marriage. Burke notes that matrimonial consent "is not just a meaning-filled decision to give oneself; it is equally a decision to accept another, which is even more meaningful."[52] The giving of self and the acceptance of the other are central concepts for the good of the spouses.

One of the often-neglected goods of marriage in terms of theological reflection is the mutual help that the spouses offer to each other. Burke notes

49. Hildebrand, *Marriage*, 57–63

50. Code of Canon Law 1055.1. "The matrimonial covenant, by which a man and a woman establish between themselves a partnership of the whole of life and which is ordered by its nature to the good of the spouses and the procreation and education of offspring, has been raised by Christ the Lord to the dignity of a sacrament between the baptized."

51. Burke, *The Theology of Marriage*, 74–77.

52. Burke, *The Theology of Marriage*, 76.

that Saint Augustine and Saint Thomas both view mutual help as part of natural development and the life of the home—it is of the natural level.[53] Burke suggests that the notion of mutual help should be absorbed into the concept of the good of the spouses. This unification of mutual help and the *bonum coniugum* is rooted in the creation of the human person as male and female. The male and the female are ordered to each other. They offer mutual help to each other in seeking the good—eternal life with God. Burke reminds, "The true good for which we are made, the good that is our destiny, is God himself."[54]

The nature of the good of the spouses is the perfection of the individual within the communion. The spouses help each other to grow in holiness and virtue in the context of an exclusive and permanent commitment which is open to the fruit of procreation. It is also, and principally, an environment in which one learns how to love. Burke states, "To learn to love demands coming out of self through firm dedication, in good times and bad, to another and to others."[55] The spousal relationship enables each of the spouses to participate in a setting of mutual self giving. The spousal relationship is a school of the Lord's service in love.

The gift of love given by each spouse, however, is not perfect.[56] In a real sense, Burke admits there is something defective about the gift. Neither of the spouses are perfect. Each of them loves imperfectly and each of them is imperfectly lovable. Aided by grace, each imperfect partner is able to make a gift of self to the other imperfect partner and accept the other even in his or her imperfection. There is an opportunity for a powerful maturing of the spouses, and this reflects what is meant by the *bonum coniugum*.

There is an important distinction between the good of the spouses and the three traditional goods of marriage provided by Saint Augustine. He proposed the goods of faithfulness, permanence, and fruitfulness; these are essential properties or goods of marriage. They belong to the institution and nature of the relationship: without them, there is no marriage.[57] The good of the spouses, on the other hand, does not refer to the institution of marriage itself, but to the growth and development of the spouses resulting from marriage. As Burke writes, "The 'good of the spouses,' we insist, is the good of learning to love, preparing for heaven, of seeking holiness."[58]

53. Burke, *Theology of Marriage*, 78–82.
54. Burke, *Theology of Marriage*, 82.
55. Burke, *Theology of Marriage*, 86.
56. Burke, *Theology of Marriage*, 86–87.
57. Burke, *Theology of Marriage*, 91–93.
58. Burke, *Theology of Marriage*, 96.

Summary of the Conjugal Bond and the Good of the Spouses

The anthropological evaluation which began this chapter describes the participants in the spousal relationship; love provides the motivation. The conjugal bond and the good of the spouses examine the nature of the relationship and the communion established through it. The bond of the spouses is intentional, sanctifying, and testimonial. The good of the spouses concerns the growth, development, and holiness of the spouses achieved through their bond. The next section moves from the nature of the bond in a spousal relationship to its effect: fruitfulness.

FRUITFULNESS AND RESPONSIBLE PARENTHOOD

The spousal relationship is fruitful. Traditionally this fruitfulness refers to the procreation and education of children. However, this fruitfulness also extends to the spiritual realm as the couple incarnates the love of Christ for the church and to the social realm as the couple lives as a community of service and caring.[59] While there are other dimensions of marital fruitfulness, this section focuses on the physical procreative aspect of children.

According to the teaching of Pope Saint John Paul II, the fruitfulness of marriage flows from the parental meaning of the body.[60] As noted earlier, the parental meaning of the body refers to the capacity of the spousal union to be fruitful. The union of spouses, following the natural cycles of nature, is open to the procreation of new life. However, there is an important distinction to be made in regard to fruitfulness. Anderson and Granados, in their work on the writings of Pope Saint John Paul II, note the difference between a product and a fruit. They write, "Whereas a product is the end result of a calculated and deliberate effort to transform the world by our own innate powers, the generation of a fruit always exceeds our native capabilities, and so is never completely subject to our choice or calculation."[61] Fruitfulness is the participation in a greater reality. A fruit is a gift and can only be received as such. This is the principle at stake in the discussion of different reproductive technologies. Many of these technological methods modify the human person, usually at the embryonic stage, from a gift to a product. The issue of fruitfulness is also compromised in the use of contraception, a topic which

---

59. For further insight on the social dimension of fruitfulness, see Rubio, *A Christian Theology of Marriage and Family*, particularly the chapters on the marriage liturgy and the vocation of Christian parents.
60. John Paul II, *Theology of the Body*, 541–42.
61. Anderson and Granados, *Called to Love*, 182.

occupies part of the final section of the Wednesday audiences of Pope Saint John Paul II.[62] Artificial contraception is a rejection of the gift in anticipation of its possibility. It denies the fullness of the spousal meaning of the body and deprives the conjugal act of its full power and meaning. The use of contraception attacks the filial meaning of the body as well, for it offers the human person a way to become less that he was created to be. It liberates instinct and desire from reason and love and shackles the person to a bondage that seeks only pleasure. It makes the gift a product. It makes the person a thing.

The blessing of fruitfulness can be both a physical and a spiritual reality. As noted earlier, not every marriage is blessed with children, yet every marriage can be a fruitful sign and presence of God's love and fidelity. Included in the aspect of fruitfulness in marriage is the notion of responsible parenthood. Pope Saint Paul VI included this in his encyclical *Humanae Vitae*.[63] The notion of responsible parenthood in marriage is a particular contribution of this encyclical. The Pope offers four different vantage points to examine this issue: biological, emotional and volitional, economic and social, and moral. A biological vision of responsible parenthood respects the laws of procreation and sexuality inherent in the nature of the human person. The emotional and volitional aspect places human emotions and innate drives under the control of reason. Responsible parenthood in regard to economic and social conditions concerns the choice of the spouses, within reason and moral precepts, to have more children or to avoid pregnancy for an indefinite or specific period of time. To these considerations the Pope adds the moral dimension that responsible parenthood is an exercise of the virtue of justice through which the spouses recognize and fulfill their duties to God, each other, themselves, their families, and society. Responsible parenthood is an act of cooperation with God and not simply an activity of the spouses.[64]

Summary of Fruitfulness and Responsible Parenthood

The spousal relationship is, by its nature and intention, fruitful. This fruitfulness flows from the complementarity of the spouses. The relationship which is motivated by love and expressed in volitional and sexual union is designed to be procreative. This procreative capacity, according to the

---

62. John Paul II, *Theology of the Body*, 617–58.
63. Paul VI, *Humanae Vitae*, 10.
64. Paul VI, *Humanae Vitae*, 10–14.

constant teaching of the church, cannot be deliberately frustrated.[65] At the same time, the capacity for physical fruitfulness must be balanced by the understanding of responsible parenthood. The notion of responsible parenthood requires open and effective communication between the spouses and each other as well as the spouses and God. This open and effective communication is lived in marital spirituality.

MARITAL SPIRITUALITY

The final aspect of the spousal relationship is marital spirituality. The nebulous notion of spirituality, particularly a spirituality rooted in the vocation of marriage, is not as well developed as the spiritualities of the religious or priestly vocations. As a true vocation, a lifelong path to holiness and personal growth and development, marriage requires a spirituality that is neither monastic or sacerdotal. Marriage is worthy of its own spirituality. This section includes an exploration of the marital spirituality of tenderness presented by Perry J. Cahall in his work, *The Mystery of Marriage: A Theology of the Body and the Sacrament*, and the marital spirituality of supernatural communion presented by Pope Francis at the conclusion of *Amoris Laetitia*.

Tenderness

The spirituality of tenderness is an important contribution to the notion of marital spirituality and is explored in this section.[66] Cahall offers the following definition as a framework for this exploration of marital spirituality: "authentic Christian spirituality is the all-encompassing effort to conform one's life more perfectly to the person of Jesus Christ, under the guidance of the Holy Spirit in the context of the ecclesial community."[67] An authentic spirituality is an activity of the whole person which reflects the inseparable connection between body and soul, creed and conduct, individual and community. Spirituality possesses a Christological goal empowered by the Spirit and supported within the ecclesial communion. These characteristics provide the foundation upon which a spirituality of marriage is built.

Cahall enumerates five components of a marital spirituality of tenderness: reverence, sacrifice, suffering, repair, and resurrection.[68] As the foun-

---

65. Paul VI, *Humanae Vitae*, 14.
66. Cahall, *Mystery of Marriage*, 344–45.
67. Cahall, *Mystery of Marriage*, 333.
68. Cahall, *Mystery of Marriage*, 345.

dational aspect of this spirituality, reverence describes the disposition of the spouses toward each other. Each spouse recognizes the full personhood and dignity of the other as a unique and precious manifestation of God's creative power. Reverence is rooted in the Christian anthropological vision of the human person as the *imago Dei*. Furthermore, this reverence flows from the recognition that the spouse is received as a gift from God in Christ. A spouse is not earned, but given. Each spouse possesses the fundamental character of a gift. Reverence is demonstrated in delicate attention and selfless love for this gift in all aspects of the marital relationship.[69]

The spirit of reverence is manifested in willingness to sacrifice. This sacrificial extension of the reverential disposition requires each spouse to sacrifice their own wants and desires, and at times needs, for the good and growth of the other. This sacrifice is an oblation modeled on the gift of Christ to the church offered on the cross. Among the many offerings presented on the altar of matrimonial spirituality is self-centeredness, which seeks fulfillment in isolation and community as a forum only for the meeting of personal desires. The sacrifice required by reverence is offered to the spouse and for the marital relationship in which the spouses participate. Sacrifice is for the good of each spouse and for the good of the spouses as a communion of persons.[70]

Reverence and sacrifice involve suffering; suffering is the third component of a marital spirituality of tenderness. Each spouse suffers for the other and for their marriage bond. The suffering of one spouse can be caused by the other, as the effects of personal sin always damage the communion of persons. More importantly, however, each spouse suffers with the other in a spirit of compassion and for the other in a spirit of communion. The spouses are united in suffering because their bond has been taken up into the Paschal Mystery. The life of Jesus Christ is manifested in their union as a married couple. They experience the suffering of self-growth, that painful metamorphosis through which the seed dies and reveals new life (cf. John 12:24). Each spouse suffers individually and in communion with the other.[71]

The fourth component of the marital spirituality of tenderness is repairing, which means constant attention and maintenance for the relationship.[72] Cahall also notes that the task of repairing can focus on the damage due to neglect. Practically, he proposes expressing mutual appreciation and esteem as part of the repairing process. An essential part of the repairing facet is

---

69. Cahall, *The Mystery of Marriage*, 345–47.
70. Cahall, *The Mystery of Marriage*, 348–53.
71. Cahall, *The Mystery of Marriage*, 353–58.
72. Cahall, *The Mystery of Marriage*, 358–63.

forgiveness. He states, "There is no greater way for a married couple to be tender with each other than to offer forgiveness and mercy to each other."[73]

The capstone of the spirituality of tenderness is resurrection. Cahall explains that through reverence, sacrifice, suffering, and repairing, the continual resurrection of the relationship is possible. This also includes regular participation in the sacraments, a key feature of any Catholic spirituality. As the spouses unite themselves to the Risen Lord, the bond of their marriage is strengthened.[74]

The spirituality of tenderness which includes dimensions of reverence, sacrifice, suffering, repairing, and resurrection explores the practical and pastoral implications of the Catholic vision of the marriage. This spirituality, rooted in the relationship between the spouses, is complemented by the spirituality of supernatural communion which begins with the relationship between the couple and God.

Supernatural Communion

The final section of *Amoris Laetitia* concerns marital spirituality based in supernatural communion.[75] Central to this idea is the notion that the Trinity dwells in the relationship of the couple, and not simply in each spouse. The bond between them is the temple of God.[76] Therefore, the family is not a distraction from a life of holiness; the family is a path to holiness.[77]

The spirituality of marriage, according to Pope Francis, is lived in thousands of small gestures.[78] The events and activities of daily life are the opportunities for sanctification. Among these activities, the Holy Father recommends family prayer and the celebration of popular piety. Pope Francis encourages participation in the Eucharist for the spouses because they will draw their strength from Christ's gift of self.

One of the chief fruits of the spirituality of marriage is the experience of belonging.[79] The spouses belong to each other in a relationship that is exclusive. They offer mutual support and assistance as they grow older. Maintaining the spirit of belonging requires a commitment to daily renewal. It also requires the recognition of the spouses' mutual belonging to the Lord. Each

73. Cahall, *Mystery of Marriage*, 363.
74. Cahall, *Mystery of Marriage*, 363–64.
75. Francis, *Amoris Laetitia*, 313–25.
76. Francis, *Amoris Laetitia*, 314.
77. Francis, *Amoris Laetitia*, 316.
78. Francis, *Amoris Laetitia*, 315.
79. Francis, *Amoris Laetitia*, 319.

spouse belongs to Christ before they belong to each other. The baptismal vocation precedes the marital. However, each spouse is a sacred gift and an image of God to the other. For this reason, Pope Francis invites the spouses to contemplate the presence of God through the eyes of Christ in each other. He says that the spouse merits the complete attention of the other.[80]

Another fruit of the spirituality of marriage is hospitality. The love within the communion of persons extends into a welcoming spirit beyond the communion of persons. In the spirit and actions of hospitality, the family is a missionary community. Pope Francis writes, "The family lives its spirituality precisely by being at one and the same time a domestic church and a vital cell for transforming the world."[81]

The Holy Father offers a final caution: the family is not a perfect community, but a community seeking perfection. Each spouse is incapable of fulfilling all of the needs, wants, and desires of the other. To expect such fulfillment from another human person is idolatry. However, the gift of grace in the sacrament of marriage offers the couple the means to walk the path to the kingdom.[82]

The spirituality of marriage presented at the conclusion of *Amoris Laetitia* recognizes the marriage bond as the temple of God and the family as the place of sanctification. It requires daily attention to the great things and the small things of life. It provides a sense of profound belonging and a community for growth. In this spirituality of supernatural communion, the family discerns both its identity and its mission.

Summary of Marital Spirituality

The spousal relationship is lived through the communion of the spouses with each other and with God. Taking these two views of marital spirituality, three common aspects are clear: identity, attention, and patient expectation. The spouses possess an identity as a dual unity called and equipped by God to care for each other, children, and the larger community. The spouses live and grow within their marital relationship through daily and loving attention to each other. Finally, the spouses allow with patient expectation the flourishing of their spouse as imperfect people striving for perfection. This concludes marital spirituality as the final aspect explored of the spousal relationship. The next section examines the analysis of Ephesians 5:21–33

---

80. Francis, *Amoris Laetitia*, 323.
81. Francis, *Amoris Laetitia*, 324.
82. Francis, *Amoris Laetitia*, 325.

by Pope Saint John Paul II as a way to summarize and unify the aspects of the spousal relationship between husband and wife.

AN EPHESIAN VISION

Following this chapter's brief anthropological evaluation, examination of love, the conjugal bond and the good of the spouses, fruitfulness and responsible parenthood, and marital spirituality, an examination of the vision of the spousal relationship presented by Pope Saint John Paul II in his examination of Ephesians 5:21–33 is appropriate.[83] His analysis of this passage offers a unifying vision of the marital relationship between husband and wife and between Christ and the Church.

If the analysis presented for the first chapters of Genesis can be considered anthropological, then the analysis presented for the fifth chapter of the Letter to the Ephesians can be characterized as matrimonial.[84] The examination of this often controversial text, Ephesians 5:21–33, concerns the relationship of the spouses individually with Christ, the relationship of the spouses as a unity with Christ, and the metaphor of Christ the Bridegroom and the church as bride. This analysis presupposes the theological reflection on the nature of the human person and the meanings of the body presented earlier. Pope Saint John Paul II also discusses the body on both the concrete level in regard to husband and wife and the metaphorical level in regard to Christ and the church. Additionally, he offers two guiding principles as hermeneutical keys to the Ephesian letter: the mystery of Christ in the divine plan and the Christian vocation of living in communion with Christ and the community.[85]

The passage under consideration begins with an invitation to the spouses for mutual subjection or subordination to Christ. The relationship of the spouses together on the concrete level is predicated on their relationship to Christ individually. The spouses are reciprocally related to each other, and all that follows in this passage about their relationship can only be authentically interpreted in reference to their mutual subordination to Christ. By giving themselves to Christ, they are capable of giving themselves to each other. Referencing the pastorally difficult and controversial verse

---

83. John Paul II, *Theology of the Body*, 465–529.

84. For additional and alternate perspectives on this passage see MacDonald, *Sacra Pagina Series*, vol. 17, *Colossians and Ephesians*, 324–42; Payne, "What about Headship: From Hierarchy to Equality" in *Mutual By Design*, ed. Elizabeth Beyer, 141–61; Polaski, *A Feminist Introduction to Paul*, 96–101.

85. John Paul II, *Theology of the Body*, 465–68.

about the submission of the wife to the husband, the Pope clarifies, "the author does not intend to say that the husband is the 'master' of the wife and that the interpersonal covenant proper to marriage is a contract of domination over the wife."[86] The submission can only be mutual and reciprocal. He continues, "Love excludes every kind of submission by which the wife would become a servant or slave of the husband, an object of one-sided submission."[87] The effect of the reciprocal gift and mutual submission is the maturation of the spouses and the conjugal bond.

Moving from the concrete to the metaphorical level of the body, the Pope explores the analogy of Christ and the church. These two pairings, Christ-church and husband-wife, illuminate each other. The union of Christ and the church reveals and realizes in time the mystery of salvation hidden in eternity. This is the mystery of God's eternal love and desire for union with humanity. In the Letter to the Ephesians, human marriage is called to an elevated status which participates in and presents the love of Christ the Bridegroom who gives himself completely to the church and the church who gives herself completely back to Christ.[88] Describing this spousal love, the Pope writes: "This is the redeeming, saving love with which man has been loved by God from eternity in Christ."[89] The relationship between Christ and the church is complete, total, reciprocal and mutual. This is the call for Christian spouses —to be complete, total, reciprocal, and mutual— in the sacrament of marriage.

There is a supplementary analogy included in Ephesians, Christ as Head of the body the church (Eph 5:23), which merited comment by the Pope. In the same verse the head and body analogy is said of the husband for the wife. Since all forms of domination and non-reciprocal submission were excluded, this analogy cannot be understood as an exercise of power; it can only be understood as an expression of loving unity. Christ gives himself completely to the church forming her by this gift as his bride. They form an organic unity which, while remaining two subjects, is redeeming. Christ and the church form one body; it is this one flesh union that relates this image to marriage.[90]

A critical, though less controversial, verse in this passage commands the husband to love his wife as his own body. The bridegroom is committed through love to know the bride intimately, to care for her personally, and to

---

86. John Paul II, *Theology of the Body*, 473.
87. John Paul II, *Theology of the Body*, 473.
88. John Paul II, *Theology of the Body*, 474–75.
89. John Paul II, *Theology of the Body*, 476.
90. John Paul II, *Theology of the Body*, 478–83.

reverence her completely as if she were his own body. Though called to a one flesh union, the wife does not become part of the husband. She does not lose her personhood and is not absorbed into the person of the husband. The bride remains a distinct ontological subject. She is loved by the husband *as* he loves his own body and not *because* she is his own body. The male and the female enjoy an ontological complementarity. They are capable of and called to relationship with each other. The unity or communion of marriage is a moral unity constituted by love. It is an act of generous freedom through which the spouses make a gift of themselves to the other. However, self-gift does not entail self-destruction. The husband and wife remain distinct subjects. The communion of persons created by mutual self-gift is a moral unity made possible by the spouses' ontological complementarity.[91]

The issues of reciprocity, mutuality, unity, and complementarity form the basis for the discussion of the sacramentality of marriage. As a visible sign of grace and a participation in the reality of God's life, a sacrament both reveals and redeems. The Letter to the Ephesians proposes the union of husband and wife as a concrete analogy for the love which Christ bears for the church. Through this love, Christ cleanses and nourishes his bride and makes of her a sign and an agent of his grace. She receives her life and her identity from him. This is a point of great dissimilarity with human marriage, for the wife receives her life, dignity, and identity from God, not from her husband. However, in the communion of marriage, both spouses grow in life, dignity, and identity through their relationship with each other. The spouses are consecrated agents of grace for each other. They are suitable helpers for each other in their development as persons and as Christians. The communion of persons that is marriage offers a tangible sign of the eternal love that God has for creation and Christ has for the church. The sacramental nature of marriage is both a strength for the spouses and a testimony to the church and the world.

The characteristics of mutuality, reciprocity, unity and complementarity, and sacramentality offer an insight into the mystery of marriage as an analogy for the mystery of Christ's love for the church. These aspects presented by Pope Saint John Paul II in his examination of Ephesians 5:21–33 provide the foundation upon which the fruitfulness of marriage can flourish.

Summary of An Ephesian Vision

The vision of marriage presented in Ephesians 5:21–33 and analyzed by Pope Saint John Paul II offers a synthesis of the characteristics of the spousal

---

91. John Paul II, *Theology of the Body*, 483–87.

relationship explored in this chapter. Building upon the anthropological foundation, the examination of this passage summarizes the matrimonial implications of Pope Saint John Paul II's presentation in the Wednesday Audiences from September, 1979 through November, 1984. The Ephesian vision unites the several facets of the spousal relationship explored in this chapter.

CONCLUSION

This chapter presents several facets of the spousal relationship. The anthropological evaluation demonstrates that the human person possesses the capacity for physical and spiritual communion. This communion is made possible by the asymmetrical reciprocity of sexual difference and is motivated by love. The love which motivates the spousal relationship is protected by and grows within the context of the conjugal bond and leads to the good of the spouses. The spousal relationship is fruitful through the gift of children and the witness of loving fidelity. As a continuous living reality, the spousal relationship is supported by a spirituality of marriage that focuses on identity, careful attention, and patient expectation. Through his examination of Ephesians 5:21–33, Pope Saint John Paul II presents an overview of the spousal relationship between husband and wife and Christ and the church.

The spousal relationship is the typical manifestation of *mutual kenotic vulnerability*. Marriage is a mutual relationship based on the complementarity of the spouses and the consent that each of them offers. It is a kenotic relationship because it involves a gift of self on the part of each spouse; this gift is motivated by and expressed through love. Vulnerability, that is the possibility of both harm and flourishing, is a necessary condition of fruitfulness. As the spouses are vulnerable to each other, the depth of their mutual kenotic gift is deepened.

This first chapter focused on the spousal relationship between husband and wife. Chapter 2 applies the characteristics of the nuptial relationship between husband and wife to the spousal relationship between the priest and the church.

Chapter 2

The Spousal Relationship

Priest and Church

ON MARCH 25, 1992 Pope Saint John Paul II issued his Apostolic Exhortation *Pastores Dabo Vobis* which concerns the formation of priests. More than simply a document on the conduct and course of studies to be followed in Catholic seminaries, *Pastores Dabo Vobis* presents the heart of Pope Saint John Paul II's vision of the ministerial priesthood. In this document, he introduces into magisterial teaching the spousal dimension of the priesthood.[1] Earlier suggested in his Apostolic Letter *Mulieris Dignitatem, On the Dignity and Vocation of Women*, the notion of the priest as a bridegroom of the church was made explicit in *Pastores Dabo Vobis*.[2] Pope St. John Paul II writes, "The priest is called to be the living image of Jesus Christ, the spouse of the Church," and "the priest stands in this spousal relationship with regard to the community."[3]

In order to more deeply explore this sacerdotal-ecclesial relationship, the basic characteristics of the spousal relationship seen in chapter 1 will be applied and examined. This chapter provides an overview of the ministerial priesthood in order to contextualize the spousal dimension. A brief

1. John Paul II, *Pastores Dabo Vobis*, 4.
2. John Paul II, *Mulieris Dignitatem*, 26. See also *Pastores Dabo Vobis*, 22.
3. John Paul II, *Pastores Dabo Vobis*, 22.

examination of the model relationship between Christ the Bridegroom and the church as bride precedes the exploration of the dual participation in the one priesthood of Christ, the motivating charity, the sacramental bond, fruitfulness and spirituality. Additionally, through the examination of these facets, the spousal union between the priest and the church can be seen as a relationship of *mutual kenotic vulnerability*.

As chapter 1 focused on the relationship between husband and wife, this chapter concerns the relationship between the priest and the church. The spousal dimension proposed by Pope Saint John Paul II flows from the relational aspects of his view of priesthood. A brief overview of the ministerial priesthood offers a context from which to explore the nuptial dimension and is provided in the next section.

AN OVERVIEW OF THE MINISTERIAL PRIESTHOOD

The Preface for the Chrism Mass proclaims, "Christ not only adorns with a royal priesthood the people he has made his own, but with a brother's kindness he also chooses men to become sharers in his sacred ministry by the laying on of hands."[4] The priesthood is, first and foremost, a gift that Christ has willed for his church. This gift "renders tangible the actual work of Christ, the Head, and gives witness to the fact that Christ has not separated himself from his Church; rather He continues to vivify her through his everlasting priesthood."[5] The ministerial priesthood and the ministerial priest are a gift that the community cannot create or give unto itself, but must receive it by means of episcopal succession going back to the Apostles.[6] Through the ministry of priests, the church lives the foundational obedience to the command of Christ to proclaim the Gospel and celebrate the Eucharist.[7] Constitutive of the nature of the church, the gift of the ministerial priesthood is a multifaceted relationship and has Trinitarian, Christological, pneumatological, and ecclesial dimensions.

Through the Sacrament of Baptism, each Christian is received into the communion of the Blessed Trinity. Sacred ordination places a man in

---

4. *Roman Missal*, "Preface of the Chrism Mass."

5. Congregation for the Clergy, *Directory on the Ministry and Life of Priests*, 1. Hereafter *Directory*. On February 11, 2013, the Congregation for the Clergy issued a new edition of the *Directory*. However, it was not widely published, is not available from the United States Conference of Catholic Bishops, and as of October 2020, there is no English translation of this work on the website of the Congregation for the Clergy. For these reasons, all references in this work are to the 1994 edition of the *Directory*.

6. See John Paul II, *Ecclesia de Eucharistia*, 29.

7. John Paul II, *Pastores Dabo Vobis*, 1.

a particular kind of relationship. This relationship is born of the Father's love, shares in the sacrificial identity and salvific mission of the Son, and is sacramentally united to the ministry of Jesus by the power of the Holy Spirit. In consequence of this, "the priest must live this relationship in an intimate and personal manner, in a dialogue of adoration and love with the three divine Persons, conscious that he has received this gift for the service of all."[8] This is an important point of reflection for those who exercise the sacred ministry. The priesthood is not a gift given for the domination of others; it is given for the service and benefit of all. Of particular interest here is that, with the exception of Holy Communion consecrated through his ministry, the priest is sacramentally unavailable to himself. He cannot be the direct beneficiary of the gift that he has received. It is impossible for him to bestow absolution on himself or to anoint himself. He has received the gift of ordination for the service others.

The Christological dimension stems from the nature of sacred ordination itself. Through the sacrament of Holy Orders in the presbyteral degree, a man is configured at the core of his being to Christ the High Priest. He is "endowed with a 'spiritual power' which is a share in the authority with which Jesus Christ guides the Church through his Spirit."[9] The priest is made a sharer in the mission and ministry of Jesus Christ in such a way that he is able to act in his person [*in persona Christi capitis*], and therefore "becomes the minister of the essential sacramental actions, transmits the truths necessary for salvation and cares for the People of God, leading them toward sanctity."[10] Clarifying the meaning of *in persona Christi*, Pope Saint John Paul II wrote that it "means more than offering 'in the name of' or 'in the place of' Christ; *in persona* means in specific sacramental identification with 'the eternal High Priest.'"[11] Therefore priestly ordination creates a relationship whose level of intimacy is such that a man hands over to Christ for his use not only his will, body, and identity, but his personal pronoun—so when this man says, "I absolve you" and "This is my body," it is the Lord Jesus who acts.

The pneumatological dimension, that is the relationship of the priest to the Holy Spirit, centers around the sacramental character received in ordination. By the power of the Holy Spirit, the priest is configured to "always be the minister of Christ and the Church."[12] The character is not something

---

8. Congregation for the Clergy, *Directory*, 5.
9. John Paul II, *Pastores Dabo Vobis*, 21.
10. Congregation for the Clergy, *Directory*, 7.
11. John Paul II, *Letters to My Brother Priests*, 8.
12. Congregation for the Clergy, *Directory*, 8.

that the priest can give up, lose, or have taken from him. A priest can, for grave reasons, be relieved of the obligations of the ministerial priesthood, or can have his faculties (legal permission to function as a priest) taken away by disciplinary decree. However, a priest can never be "un-ordained." A priest is a priest forever because of the indelible sacramental character. In addition to this indelible character, the Holy Spirit confers on the priest and directs him in the "prophetic task of announcing and explaining, with authority, the Word of God."[13] United to the Holy Spirit in the celebration of the Eucharist and the Sacraments, the priest "finds the strength to guide the community entrusted to him and to maintain it in the unity wanted by the Lord."[14] By the power of the Holy Spirit, the priest is configured to Christ the Lord and consecrated as a minister to and for the church.

Lastly, the ecclesial dimension of priestly ministry is of central importance for this book. Flowing from the relationship of the priest to the persons of the Blessed Trinity, the priest's relationship to the church is one of deep intimacy. Configured to Christ the Lord, the priest is inserted into the relationship between Christ and the church. The spousal relationship between Christ and the church was expounded in the fifth chapter of the letter to the Ephesians. It is loving, sacrificing, sanctifying, and unifying. The priest shares in this spousal relationship with the church and he must "be faithful to the Bride and almost like living icon of Christ the Spouse render fruitful the multi-form donation of Christ to his Church."[15] In his union with Christ the Spouse or Bridegroom of the Church, the priest is "called to the act of supernatural love . . . consecrating to [the Church] all his energies and giving himself with pastoral charity in a continuous act of generosity."[16] The spousal character of the priest's relationship to the church impacts every aspect of his identity and ministry. The priest shares in the identity of Christ the Bridegroom.

As the priest shares in the identity and mission of Christ, the priest also shares in Christ's mission in the church. Liturgically, this total gift of self and consecration for mission is seen by the prostration during the ordination rite. In a gesture filled with emotion, memory, and prayer, the man to be ordained ritually symbolizes both his total openness to the Holy Spirit and his total submission before God. Pope Saint John Paul II writes, "the one about to receive Holy Orders prostrates himself completely and rests his forehead on the church floor, indicating in this way his *complete willingness*

---

13. Congregation for the Clergy, *Directory*, 9.
14. Congregation for the Clergy, *Directory*, 11.
15. Congregation for the Clergy, *Directory*, 13.
16. Congregation for the Clergy, *Directory*, 13.

to undertake the ministry being entrusted to him."[17] In this gesture at ordination and in every day that follows, a spousal union is formed and celebrated as the priest places himself totally at the loving service of the church, the Bride of Jesus Christ.

The overview provided in this section presents the ministerial priesthood as a multi-dimensional relationship. The priest does not exist in isolation, but finds his identity and mission in communion. One dimension of this communion, and critical for this book, is the ecclesial dimension, the relationship between the priest and the church. The model for this relationship is the union between Christ and the church and will be explored in the next section.

THE MODEL RELATIONSHIP

The spousal union between Christ and the church is the model for the priest's nuptial relationship. This section provides a brief biblical examination of Jesus as Bridegroom and the church as bride of Christ.

The image of Jesus as Bridegroom can be examined from several vantage points. First, the bridegroom-bride metaphor for the relationship between the Lord and the people of Israel is often utilized in the prophetic writings. Hosea 2:4–25 depicts the spousal relationship along with the infidelity of Israel in graphic detail. Mark Tait comments that this passage "uses nuptial symbolism to indicate the wrathful but enduring love of Yahweh for his people."[18] The prophet Jeremiah alludes to Israel as an unfaithful wife (Jer 3:20), but also promises a new and renewed covenant (Jer 31:31–34). Isaiah describes the nuptial love of the Lord for Israel (Isa 54:1–10). Song of Songs abounds with spousal imagery (1:4; 1:7; 5:16; 6:3). Summarizing the Old Testament expectation Brant Pitre writes, "Above all, they are waiting for the coming of the Bridegroom of God of Israel, who will forgive their sins and unite himself to them in an everlasting marriage covenant."[19] The image of the bridegroom in the prophetic writings anticipates the appearance of the Bridegroom in the Gospels. The first vantage point of Jesus as Bridegroom is as fulfilling the prophets.

The Bridegroom for whom the prophets hoped is Jesus Christ. The second dimension of Jesus as Bridegroom is his own claim to the title and

---

17. John Paul II, *Gift and Mystery*, 43–44. The prostration by the priest is repeated every year on Good Friday. For analysis see Office for the Liturgical Celebrations of the Supreme Pontiff, "Priest and the Paschal Triduum."

18. Tait, *Jesus, the Divine Bridegroom*, 137.

19. Pitre, *Jesus the Bridegroom*, 27.

the reference of John the Baptist. In Mark 2:19 Jesus essentially claims the title of Bridegroom for himself: "Can the wedding guests fast while the bridegroom is with them? As long as they have the bridegroom with them they cannot fast." In his parable of the Ten Virgins (Matt 25:1–12) Jesus is presented as the bridegroom who is long delayed.[20] In John 3:28–30, John the Baptist refers to Jesus as the bridegroom, specifically as the one who has the bride. John the Baptist regards himself as the friend of the bridegroom, the one who will rejoice to hear the voice of the bridegroom. In his words and actions, John the Baptist indicates that Jesus is the Bridegroom.[21] This second aspect of Jesus as Bridegroom reflects the claim and the reference of John the Baptist.

The third aspect of Jesus as Bridegroom is demonstrated in symbolic actions. Two scenes in the Gospel of John are particularly significant. The first is the wedding at Cana and the second in the encounter with the woman at the well. At the wedding at Cana (John 2:1–11), Jesus takes on the role of the bridegroom by providing the wine.[22] Pitre states that providing good and abundant wine harkens back to the messianic banquet prophesied by Isaiah (25:6–8). As Pitre explains, when Jesus provides miraculous wine at the wedding feast, he reveals himself as both the messiah and the bridegroom of Israel.[23] Brendan Byrne comments that the abundance of wine "signals the presence here at this Galilean village wedding of Israel's Bridegroom."[24]

The giving of wine seen at Cana in the Gospel of John is also viewed in the Upper Room in the synoptic Gospels (Matt 26:27–28; Mark 14:23–24; Luke 22:17–20). At the Last Supper, with the inauguration of a new covenant in blood, Jesus refers to the new covenant prophesied by Jeremiah which signifies a marriage covenant. Pitre further notes that celebrating this covenantal meal with his disciples indicates that the disciples represent the bride of God.[25] He concludes by stating, "By means of the this new covenant, Jesus reveals that *he himself* is the true Bridegroom, and the new Israel that will be established through his disciples is the bride of God."[26] The wedding banquet of the Last Supper is consummated in the complete and total gift of self in love given by Jesus on the cross.[27]

20. Tait, *Jesus, the Divine Bridegroom*, 254.
21. Tait, *Jesus, the Divine Bridegroom*, 259–62.
22. Tait, *Jesus, the Divine Bridegroom*, 263–64.
23. Pitre, *Jesus the Bridegroom*, 43–45.
24. Byrne, *Life Abounding*, 53.
25. Pitre, *Jesus the Bridegroom*, 46–51.
26. Pitre, *Jesus the Bridegroom*, 51.
27. For an analysis of the Eucharistic implications of this nuptial banquet see John

The meeting with the woman at the well (John 4:1–42) provides an important connection between the Bridegroom and the bride. Wells were often places where potential spouses met each other.[28] Additionally, the pattern of a foreign male meeting a woman at a well leading to a betrothal is seen in the Pentateuch.[29] Pitre summarizes, "Jesus' encounter with the Samaritan woman at the well is remarkably similar to the encounter between Jacob, the patriarch of Israel, and Rachael, the matriarch of Israel."[30] The scene includes the offer of living water, possibly referring to a gift given by the bridegroom to the bride.[31] With the well as a setting and the offer of living water, this scene depicts an image of Jesus as the Bridegroom.

Intimately related to the notion of Jesus as Bridegroom is the image of the church as bride. The church is the relational partner to Christ. The church as bride is introduced in the New Testament in 2 Corinthians 11:2 where Paul writes, "For I am jealous of you with the jealousy of God, since I betrothed you to one husband to present you as a chaste virgin to Christ." Raymond F. Collins clarifies that for the Corinthian community, Paul "initiated the marital relationship with Christ through his preaching of the gospel."[32] The fifth chapter of the Letter to the Ephesians (5:21–33), which was examined in chapter 1, abounds with ecclesial bridal imagery. Further examples of bridal imagery are seen in Revelation.[33] In Revelation 19:7–8, the wedding feast of the Lamb is announced and the bride wears a bright garment whose linen material represents "the righteous deeds of the holy ones." In Revelation 22, the heavenly Jerusalem is referenced as the bride of the Lamb. Additionally, Revelation 22:17 states, "The Spirit and the bride say, 'Come.' Let the hearer say, 'Come.' Let the one who thirsts come forward, and the one who wants it receive the gift of life-giving water." In this verse, the bride is depicted as one who receives living water. The preceding verses noted in this paragraph provide biblical witness to the image of the church as bride.

In his doctoral dissertation, Andrew Lichtenwalner summarizes six characteristics of the church as the bride of Christ. First, the church possesses both holiness and beauty. Second, she is subordinate to Christ, receiving her life, identity, and mission from him. Third, the church is receptive

Paul II, *Mulieris Dignitatem*, 26.
    28. Pitre, *Jesus the Bridegroom*, 59–62.
    29. Schneiders, *Revelatory Text*, 187.
    30. Pitre, *Jesus the Bridegroom*, 62.
    31. Pitre, *Jesus the Bridegroom*, 70–72.
    32. Collins, *Second Corinthians*, 213.
    33. Rev 19:7–8; 21:2, 9; 22:17.

and responsive to the love of Christ. She receives the gift of Christ's love, responds in love, and participates in his salvific will and mission. Fourth, the church is fruitful, bearing, and nurturing the children of the reign of God. Fifth, she is both a historical reality as a people on pilgrimage and an eschatological reality whose full manifestation will only be revealed at the consummation of the world. Finally, the church as bride is a body of the sanctified which becomes an instrument of sanctification. She is holy and she radiates holiness.[34]

Summary

Jesus Christ is the Bridegroom of the church. This is evidenced in the scriptures as Jesus fulfills the expectation of the prophets, claims the title for himself, and symbolically participates in the actions of a bridegroom. The church receives and reciprocates the love of the Bridegroom. In this brief exposition, the union of Christ and the church is shown as a relationship of *mutual kenotic vulnerability*, meaning that the relationship is constituted by the consent of both parties, involves a gift of self or self-emptying, and both parties are open to the possibility of harm or flourishing. Christ gives himself completely to the church sharing his life, identity, spirit, mission, body, and blood with his bride. The church responds by receiving these gifts, cherishing them, and giving herself back to Christ. The union of Christ and the church is fruitful in adoration, praise, thanksgiving, mission and holiness. This examination of the spousal union between Christ and the church shows how the relationship is the perfect model for the priest's nuptial union with the church, the bride of Jesus Christ. In the next section the relationship between the priest and the faithful of the church will be explored and examined.

A DUAL PARTICIPATION

Modeled on the spousal relationship between Jesus and the church, the priest lives in an analogous nuptial relationship with the church. This section explores one of the foundational facets of the priest-church relationship. The anthropological evaluation in chapter 1 explored the concept of asymmetrical reciprocity as an essential condition for nuptiality. The spousal relationship between husband and wife is possible because of the reciprocity inherent in sexual difference. The two expressions of human personhood,

---

34. Lichtenwalner, "Church as the Bride of Christ," 70–71.

male or female, are ordered to each other to form a dual unity which possesses the capacity for fruitfulness. Analogously, in the relationship between the priest and the church, asymmetrical reciprocity is manifested in the two participations in the one priesthood of Christ: royal and ministerial. This section examines the characteristics and relational nature of the participation in the priesthood of Christ. In *Lumen Gentium, The Dogmatic Constitution on the Church*, the Second Vatican Council teaches that in the one priesthood of Christ there are two complementary participations.[35] These two participations do not reflect degrees of union with the priesthood of Christ; they are different in essence. There is no higher or lower participation. They are equal manifestations of the one priesthood of Christ. The two modes of participation are the common or royal priesthood of the baptized and the ministerial priesthood of those ordained to presbyterate and episcopate.[36] Following the theological work of Hans Urs von Balthasar, Robert Pesarchick notes these two participations can be viewed as the self-offering by the baptized and the commissioned representation by the ordained.[37] These two participations are specifically ordered to each other, are necessary for the full manifestation of the other, and are essential for the formation of the priestly community of the church.

The common or royal priesthood is received in the sacrament of baptism. It is exercised through the reception of the sacraments, thanksgiving and prayer, self-denial and charity, and by a life of holiness. In union with the ministerial priesthood, the royal priesthood participates in the offering of the Eucharist.[38] Jean-Pierre Torrell notes two dimensions or domains of the royal priesthood: the disposition for worship and the life of grace.[39] As the sacrament of baptism imparts a permanent and relational character on the soul of the baptized, the royal priesthood is inscribed in the core of one's being. The exercise of the royal priesthood is the mission which flows from the baptismal identity.

The ministerial priesthood is received through the sacrament of holy orders in the presbyteral degree. It requires beforehand as a necessary condition the royal priesthood of the baptized, as only baptized males can receive the sacrament of holy orders in this degree. The ministerial priest acts as the only minister of certain sacraments, possesses the capacity to permanently represent Christ to the community and represent the whole community to

---

35. Vatican Council II, *Lumen Gentium*, 10.
36. John Paul II, *Pastores Dabo Vobis*, 17.
37. Pesarchick, *Trinitarian Foundation*, 249–70.
38. Vatican Council II, *Lumen Gentium*, 10.
39. Torrell, *Priestly People*, 135.

God, and acts in the name of the church. Unlike the royal priest who acts in his or her own person and own name, the ministerial priest acts in the name, in the person, and by the power of Christ. The exercise of the ministerial priesthood is the mission entrusted by sacred ordination.

The two participations in the one priesthood of Christ are interrelated and dependent upon each other. Without the ministerial priesthood, the royal priesthood cannot participate in the Eucharistic sacrifice or receive the sacraments of Reconciliation, Anointing of the Sick, and Holy Communion. Without the royal priesthood of the baptized, the ministerial priesthood has no real reason for existence. Each participation is necessary for the full actualization of the other. They can only receive their identities, accomplish their missions, and flourish in holiness through dynamic interaction with each other. As the ministerial priests are taken from among the royal priests and the royal priests receive nourishment in Word and Sacrament from the ministerial priest, these two participations live in a relationship of mutual gift. This mutual gift is fully manifested in the celebration of the Eucharist. As Paul Philbert writes, "In the liturgy, believers surrender in faith and obedience to the gift of God's Word and to the movement of the Holy Spirit."[40] The royal priests and the ministerial priests join in mutual surrender to each other and unto the Lord as a living image of the spousal relationship between Christ and his church.

SUMMARY OF A DUAL PARTICIPATION

There are two participations in the one priesthood of Christ. The royal priesthood of the baptized and the ministerial priesthood of the ordained enjoy asymmetrical reciprocity analogous to the relationship between husband and wife. These two participations are different in their essence and do not reflect greater or lesser degrees of participation in the priesthood of Christ. They are mutually related and dependent on each other for their full actualization of their identities. They are joined together most intimately in the celebration of the Eucharist. The spousal union between Christ and the church provides the origin and model for the priest's relationship with the church. The dual participation in the priesthood of Christ provides asymmetrical reciprocity which is the necessary condition for nuptiality. In the next section, two manifestations of charity, the love which motivates the relationship, will be explored.

---

40. Philbert, *Priesthood of the Faithful*, 62.

CHARITY

The spousal relationship between husband and wife is motivated by conjugal love; for the relationship between the priest and the church, two terms are utilized in this book. On the part of the priest, pastoral charity is used to describe that love by which the priest loves the church. On the part of the church and the faithful, there is no established term in magisterial teaching or systematic theology to describe how the church responds in love to the pastoral charity of Christ. Confident that such a reciprocal love exists, this book proposes the term *ecclesial charity*.[41] In this section, the pastoral charity exercised by the priest and the ecclesial charity of the faithful are examined.

Pastoral Charity

In *Pastores Dabo Vobis, I Will Give You Shepherds*, Pope Saint John Paul II follows his exposition of the spousal relationship between the priest and the church with an analysis of pastoral charity. This internal principle flows from the priest's consecration to Christ the Head and Shepherd of the church. It is a participation in the pastoral charity of Christ and guides and animates the priest's spiritual life. Pastoral charity is both a gift of the Holy Spirit and a vocational task given to the priest.[42] Thomas McGovern notes that pastoral charity "is the love proper to a pastor of souls."[43]

Summarizing the pastoral charity of Christ, Andrew Cozzens writes that "it is a sacrificial service, a love which is self-giving; it is Christ's laying down his own life for the sake of the Beloved."[44] The pastoral charity of Christ is sacrificial and spousal. According to Pope Saint John Paul II, the essential content of pastoral charity is a gift of self which is directed toward the church, meaning that the church is the recipient of the gift. This gift of self manifests the love of Christ for the church and flows from the priest's consecration and not simply from his functions.[45] Dermot Power amplifies this notion: "In this gift of self to the Church, the priest is drawn into that love of the Church, both in its universal aspect and in that part of it that is

---

41. I am grateful to Dr. Carmina Chapp of Saint Joseph's College of Maine for her counsel in the selection of this term.
42. John Paul II, *Pastores Dabo Vobis*, 23.
43. McGovern, *Priestly Identity*, 60.
44. Cozzens, "Imago Vivens Iesu Christi Sponsi Ecclesiae," 234.
45. See Congregation for the Clergy, *Directory*, 43 which cautions that a purely functional understanding of priestly ministry can lead to emptiness in the heart and life of the priest.

entrusted to him, with a love analogous to the deep love of a husband for his wife."⁴⁶ The spousal aspect of the priest's pastoral charity is directed toward the church in her universal, particular, and parochial expressions; it is not simply a general charity. The *Directory* notes that through pastoral charity the priest demonstrates the "total self-giving of himself to the flock with which he has been entrusted."⁴⁷ There is a specific object or recipient of the pastoral charity from each priest. There is a specific community or ministry that possesses a particular claim on his pastoral charity and ministry. While this does not reflect an exclusive commitment as does the relationship between husband and wife, the nature of pastoral charity does require a preferential option for the energy, affection, and care of the priest. Pope Saint John Paul II states that pastoral charity, "impels the priest to an ever deeper knowledge of the hopes, the needs, the problems, the sensibilities of the people to whom he ministers, taken in their specific situations, as individuals, in their families, in society and in history."⁴⁸ In his pastoral charity, the priest lives in relationship with a partner community which manifests the universal bride.

Summary of Pastoral Charity

Pastoral charity provides the motivation for the spousal relationship between the priest and the church. It is rooted in Christ's love for the church, which is both sacrificial and spousal. The priest participates in the pastoral charity of Christ and receives this particular love as a gift of the Holy Spirit and a vocational task. This love is directed toward the church in general and toward a specific community of the faithful entrusted to the priest. Pastoral charity moves the priest to an ever deeper and intimate knowledge of his community. As Andrew Cozzens writes, "The spousal character of the priest's self-gift on behalf of the Church is discovered in pastoral charity."⁴⁹

Ecclesial Charity

Ecclesial charity, the new term proposed in this book, is the manner in which the church responds in love to the pastoral charity of Christ. "The

---

46. Power, *Spiritual Theology of the Priesthood*, 107. See also Cozzens, "Imago Vivens Iesu Christi Sponsi Ecclesiae," 234; McGovern, *Priestly Identity*, 62.

47. Congregation for the Clergy, *Directory*, 43.

48. John Paul II, *Pastores Dabo Vobis*, 70.

49. Cozzens, "Imago Vivens Iesu Christi Sponsi Ecclesiae," 236.

Church, as the spouse of Jesus Christ, wishes to be loved by the priest in the total and exclusive manner in which Jesus Christ her head and spouse loved her."[50] As it is the wish of the church to be loved, the church desires to love in return. Pastoral charity describes the love by which Christ loves the church and by extension the priest does the same; in this book, the term *ecclesial charity* describes the corresponding love of the church and all of the baptized. Ecclesial charity is the love by which the church loves Christ, the faithful love the church, and the royal priesthood of the baptized receives and reciprocates pastoral charity. Ecclesial charity is the love proper to the royal priesthood—it animates the life of the faithful in their offering of the Eucharist, reception of the sacraments, life of holy witness, charity and self-denial, and thanksgiving and prayer.

Ecclesial charity can be examined using the three meanings of the body proposed by Pope Saint John Paul II and examined in chapter 1. As the three meanings of the body are filial, spousal, and parental, analogously the three dimensions of ecclesial charity are receptive, unitive, and fruitful. Ecclesial charity is receptive in that it derives its origin from the pastoral charity of Christ. Revealed in the fifth chapter of Ephesians, the church receives her life from Christ her Head; her existence is a gift. The identity of the church is received from the prior action of Christ. In the life of each of the faithful, ecclesial charity is received as a gift from outside themselves; it is sacramentally infused in the waters of baptism. The receptive dimension of ecclesial charity, through which Christian identity and the royal priesthood are conferred, prepares for the exercise of the unitive dimension.

Ecclesial charity is unitive. It is the loving response to pastoral charity, and it motivates the participation of the faithful in the offering of Eucharist and the reception of the sacraments. While it could be posited that these sacrificial and sacramental participations exercise the receptive dimension, it seems that this would negate the celebration of the sacraments as a communal celebration. Communal means that the celebration of the sacraments involves at least two persons: the recipient and the minister. A person is not simply baptized, absolved, or anointed. A person is baptized, absolved, or anointed by someone else.[51] Sacramental celebrations are unitive acts; they are exercises of the royal and ministerial participations of the priesthood of Christ and are expressions of ecclesial and pastoral charity. The unitive dimension of ecclesial charity manifested principally in the celebration of the Eucharist and the sacraments equips and enables the fruitful dimension.

---

50. John Paul II, *Pastores Dabo Vobis*, 29.
51. For both absolution and anointing, the only minister is a validly ordained priest.

Ecclesial charity is fruitful in manifold ways. The love received in baptism, which is experienced, strengthened, and cherished in unitive celebrations, pours forth in praise and thanksgiving, self-denial and charity, and the witness of a holy life. Ecclesial charity is fruitful in the deepened bond of the faithful with the church in her universal, particular, and parochial expressions. Ecclesial charity is fruitful in every apostolic work of the prophetic mission of the baptized and is demonstrated in a multiplicity of charitable works. Ecclesial charity is evangelically fruitful because it animates a life of holiness and "holiness is the most attractive face of the Church."[52]

Summary of Ecclesial Charity

Ecclesial charity is the term proposed in this book to describe the love by which the church and the faithful love Christ. It is the love proper to the royal priesthood of the baptized and can be explored in its receptive, unitive, and fruitful dimensions. Ecclesial charity is receptive in that it originates as a gift from Christ. Ecclesial charity is unitive in relationship to the pastoral charity of the ministerial priesthood in Eucharistic and sacramental celebrations. Flowing from its union with pastoral charity in those sacramental celebrations, ecclesial charity is fruitful in a plethora of evangelical, apostolic, and charitable works. Ecclesial charity motivates one's desire to experience and share the love of Christ.

Summary of Charity

In the spousal relationship between the priest and the church, two terms are utilized to describe the love between them: pastoral charity and ecclesial charity. While conjugal love describes the love of the husband for the wife and the wife for the husband, pastoral charity and ecclesial charity describe those loving realities in the priest-church relationship. Pastoral charity is rooted in the love of Christ for the church and is received in priestly ordination as both a gift to the priest and a vocational task. The recipient of pastoral charity is the church in her universal, particular, and parochial expressions. Ecclesial charity is received in baptism, animates the life of the faithful, and is the love proper to the royal priesthood. It has receptive, unitive, and fruitful dimensions. Through the exercise of ecclesial charity, the faithful participate in the offering of the Eucharist, receive the sacraments, and live a life of faith and love. Charity animates the relationship between

---

52. Francis, *Gaudete et Exultate*, 9.

the priest and the church. The next section explores the sacramental bond in which the relationship abides.

A SACRAMENTAL BOND

The relationship between the priest and the church, which is animated by charity, abides in a sacramental bond. Analogous to the conjugal bond between husband and wife, this sacramental bond is permanent and relational. As noted in chapter 1, the bond is a source of grace within the communion of marriage and a source of blessing beyond the spouses. In the relationship between the priest and the church, the sacramental character received in ordination corresponds to the conjugal bond of marriage. Jean Galot and David L. Toups provide a complementary analysis of this sacerdotal character.

Jean Galot

In his work *Theology of the Priesthood*, Galot enumerates six aspects of the sacramental character received in priestly ordination.[53] The sacramental character is spiritual and indelible, relational, a mark of consecration, enables conformity of life to Christ, confers a share in the mission, and effects a permanent relationship to the church. As a spiritual and indelible mark, the priestly character is an ontological reality imprinted upon the soul of the recipient which can never be repeated or removed. The relational aspect, as Galot explains, refers primarily to the priest's relationship to God. He writes, "The character is first and foremost a relationship to God, to the Father, who, first through Christ, then through priests, seeks to reveal himself and bring his own action to bear upon the world."[54] Flowing from the priest's relationship to God, the sacramental character is a mark of consecration. The priest is set apart (that is, consecrated), both as a minister of Christ and a servant of humanity. The priest cannot be an exclusively cultic figure nor wholly an agent of charitable social service.[55] To the extent that he incarnates both dimensions, the priest lives the fifth aspect of his sacramental character—conformity to Christ. By sacred ordination, the priest is configured to Christ the Shepherd. Conformity to Christ means that the ontological reality of indelible spiritual consecration manifests in the life of the priest. The life of the priest serves as a living image of the Good Shepherd. While

---

53. Galot, *Theology of the Priesthood*, 195–212.
54. Galot, *Theology of the Priesthood*, 204.
55. Galot, *Theology of the Priesthood*, 204–5.

the character is spiritual, indelible, relational, and consecratory at the moment of ordination, conformity to Christ develops over time. Galot notes, "The priest cannot act consistently with what he is unless he lets himself be permeated ever more deeply by the spirit of the gospel."[56] The final two aspects of the sacramental character provide the locus in which the priest's conformity to Christ can flourish.

The final aspects of the priestly character, according to Galot, concern a share in Christ's mission and a share in Christ's relationship to the church. The sacramental character imparts a specific participation in the mission of Christ. The priest receives the capacity to proclaim the word, lead divine worship through the Eucharist and the sacraments, and shepherd the community. Galot is emphatic that the priestly character cannot be reduced to ritual functions.[57] The radiation of the priestly character extends beyond the walls of the sanctuary. Sharing in the mission of Christ is accomplished only through the charity of Christ. The priestly character imparts a power for mission, yet this power can only be authentically exercised in love and service. To do otherwise is to fail in conformity and betray the consecration.[58]

Galot concludes his analysis of the priestly character by noting that it establishes a permanent relationship with the church. Each day in the life of the priest and all of the days of the priest's life belong to the service of the church. She has an exclusive claim on him which he freely accepted in ordination.[59] In the same way that the husband and wife enter into a permanent bond, the priest lives out his consecration and grows in conformity to Christ through his permanent and loving relationship with the Church.

Having concluded the analysis of the priestly character according to Galot, the next section examines the theological contribution of David L. Toups. These two authors offer complementary perspectives which enable a fuller understanding of the dimensions of the priestly sacramental character.

David L. Toups

Writing nearly twenty-five years after Galot, David L. Toups proposes six related but slightly different characteristics of the priestly character. Toups posits permanence, acting in the person of Christ, acting in the person of the church, presence and authority as a gift, the avoidance of functionalism,

---

56. Galot, *Theology of the Priesthood*, 207.
57. Galot, *Theology of the Priesthood*, 209.
58. Galot, *Theology of the Priesthood*, 210.
59. Galot, *Theology of the Priesthood*, 211.

and the need for ongoing formation.⁶⁰ When describing permanence, Toups includes the indelible and spiritual mark which imparts a lifelong commitment to Christ and his church. He notes, "The repercussions of this permanent and loving relationship follow analogously along the lines of a marital relationship."⁶¹ There is a spousal dimension to the priestly character. The priest enters into a loving relationship with the church, and according to Toups, ignoring this spousal dimension could undermine the priest's fulfillment in ministry and life.⁶²

The two characteristics of acting in the person of Christ and acting in the person of the Church are intimately related.⁶³ The priest acts *in persona Christi* in the celebration of the sacraments. He is empowered to act in the name and person of Christ to heal, restore, reconcile, and feed. The priest acts *in persona Ecclesiae* as a consequence of his configuration to Christ. He prays in the name of the whole church. Following the spousal analogy, the priest speaks to the bride in the person of Christ and for (or, better, with) the bride in the person of the church.⁶⁴

The fourth characteristic concerns the gift of priestly presence and authority to the church.⁶⁵ Toups discusses the ministry of preaching, shepherding, and healing under this heading. He notes that the preaching ministry makes considerable claims on the time and energy of the priest. It requires both receptivity to the word and the needs of the community. Preaching also requires priestly generosity in sharing words of life and hope with the church.⁶⁶ What is proclaimed in preaching is lived in the act of shepherding. The priest dwells in the community and seeks to know the flock. He seeks out the lost and heals the wounded. The ministry of healing is extended in anointing, reconciliation, and prayer. The sacramental character enables the priest to be permanently receptive to Christ and permanently capable of serving the church in the exercise of his authority and presence.⁶⁷

---

60. Toups, *Reclaiming Our Priestly Character*, 133.
61. Toups, *Reclaiming Our Priestly Character*, 137.
62. Toups, *Reclaiming Our Priestly Character*, 145.
63. Toups, *Reclaiming Our Priestly Character*, 149–67. For further analysis of the *in persona Christi* and *in persona Ecclesiae*, see Torrell, *Priestly People*, 142–51.
64. Particularly in the celebration of the Eucharist and the Liturgy of the Hours, the priest speaks on behalf of the Ecclesial Bride. However, as the priest speaks the words provided by the church, it seems more appropriate to say that the priest speaks "with" rather than "for" the bride.
65. Toups, *Reclaiming Our Priestly Character*, 167–75.
66. Toups, *Reclaiming Our Priestly Character*, 168–70.
67. Toups, *Reclaiming Our Priestly Character*, 170–75.

The final two characteristics of the priestly character according to Toups reflect two needs. The first is the need to avoid functionalism; he cautions against two manifestations of this destructive notion. The first denies the ontological identity and relationality of the priest and the second forgets the spiritual nature of the priesthood in the light of overwhelming responsibilities.[68] The remedy for functionalism is found in the final characteristic: the need for ongoing formation. The priesthood is a multi-dimensional relationship and must receive continual attention and maintenance. Ongoing formation allows the priest to be renewed in his conformity to Christ and his love for the church.[69]

The six characteristics presented by David L. Toups are rooted in relationality. Published sixteen years after the promulgation of *Pastores Dabo Vobis*, this work reflects the influence of the relational vision of the priesthood promoted by Pope Saint John Paul II. Toups contributes an additional relational exploration of the sacramental character received in priestly ordination.

Summary of *A Sacramental Bond*

The writings of Jean Galot and David L. Toups offer an insightful analysis of the priestly sacramental character. Concluding this section, there are several points to be affirmed. First, the sacramental character received in ordination is permanent and relational. The character possesses the same dimensions explored earlier in the section on the ministerial priesthood: trinitarian, christological, pneumatological, and ecclesial. The priest is configured by the will of the Father, to the Son, through the power of the Holy Spirit. The sacramental character effects a permanent consecration to Christ and enables conformity to life of the gospel. Second, through this sacramental character, the priest is empowered to act in the person of Christ and in the person of the church. The priest lives in a relationship to the church which is analogous to the relationship between husband and wife. He manifests his love for the church through shepherding, healing, and preaching. Third, while the sacramental character endows this priest with certain spiritual powers, he is not an employee of the church who accomplishes certain functions; he is a permanently consecrated partner and living image of the Good Shepherd and Bridegroom.

The relationship between the priest and the church is sacramentally bonded and animated by charity. As the priest-church union is analogous to

---

68. Toups, *Reclaiming Our Priestly Character*, 175–76.
69. Toups, *Reclaiming Our Priestly Character*, 185.

the relationship between husband and wife, there is a fruitful extension of the relationship. The next section will explore the dimensions of fruitfulness in this union.

A FRUITFUL UNION

The sacramentally bonded union between the bridegroom and the bride is fruitful. Fruitfulness is a basic characteristic of the spousal relationship. Between husband and wife, it refers to the gift of children, to spiritual growth, and to communal charitable actions. In this book, the fruitfulness of the spousal union between the priest and the church is explored through four dimensions: doxological, spiritual, vocational, and homiletical. It is important to recall from chapter 1 the difference between a product and a fruit: "Whereas a product is the end result of a calculated and deliberate effort to transform the world by our own innate powers, the generation of a fruit always exceeds our native capabilities, and so is never completely subject to our choice or calculation."[70] The fruitful dimensions of the spousal relationship flow from human cooperation and divine grace.

The first fruit of the priest-church union is doxology. The praise of God pours forth when the church gathers to celebrate the sacred liturgy. Through the exercise of the royal priesthood of the baptized and the ministerial priesthood of the ordained, the church participates in Christ's self-offering to the Father. The doxological fruit is offered to God as the sacrifice of praise and thanksgiving.

The second fruit of the priest-church union is the spiritual fruit; it concerns the sanctification of the members of the community. The royal priests and the ministerial priests grow in holiness through their participation in the priesthood of Christ. When the community gathers for worship, it is a unitive act of mutual giving and receiving. The priestly participations join together in the offering of the Eucharist. As individuals gathered in a body, they receive the sacraments, offer prayer and thanksgiving, and contribute to the needs of the church and the poor. Together they are nourished with the word of God and the bread of life. Through this nourishment, the royal priests and the ministerial priests are equipped for every good work in the building up of the reign of God. The spiritual fruit overflows in the work of evangelization, catechesis, and care for the poor and the marginalized. The spiritual fruit is a source of nourishment for the faithful and a sign of witness to the world.

---

70. Anderson and Granados, *Called to Love*, 182.

A third dimension of fruitfulness is vocational. In the spousal relationship between husband and wife, this is normally children. In the priest-church relationship, this fruit is seen in priests, religious, married couples, and single persons whose vocations are nurtured in the community. In regard to vocations to the ministerial priesthood, Pope Saint John Paul writes that within each priest "is the concern which the priest should have to find, so to speak, someone to replace him in the priesthood."[71] The vocational fruit empowers the next generation to carry on the work of the Gospel.

The fourth fruit, which will be explored in much greater detail in Chapter 3, is homiletical. The homily is an expression of pastoral charity by the ministerial priest and an active reception in ecclesial charity by the royal priesthood. Adrienne Von Speyr provides a beautiful analysis of the place of the homily in the life of the priest and the community in her work *The World of Prayer*.[72] She notes that the homily is the fruit of the priest's prayer, inspires the faithful to prayer, reflects the priest as shepherd hearing the word with his flock, and is an expression of and stimulus for the union between the preacher and the community. Von Speyr writes, "Few things foster the community of prayer between the priest and the flock so much as the homily."[73] The homiletical fruit grows on the tree of unity planted in the parish garden. Preaching is a creative and unitive act within the community. While the priest is the one who speaks and reflects the word of God, he does not speak the word in isolation. The homily is a word proclaimed to and for a particular community. There is no homily without a hearer: it is the bond and fruit of a relationship.

Summary of Fruitfulness

The nuptial union between the priest and the church is fruitful. In this section, four aspects of fruitfulness were presented: doxological, spiritual, vocational, and homiletical. Through praise of God, growth in holiness, openness to the call of God, and preaching that nourishes and prunes, the community deepens its internal bond and strengthens its witness as a community of holiness.

Fruitfulness is supported through loving attention to the relationship. The final section of this chapter explores the spiritual implications for the priest of this spousal relationship.

---

71. John Paul II, *Pastores Dabo Vobis*, 74.
72. Speyr, *World of Prayer*, 183–85.
73. Speyr, *World of Prayer*, 185.

SPIRITUALITY OF THE BRIDEGROOM

There are manifold ways to describe priestly spirituality. Various facets of ministry provide vistas for examination and engagement in the priest's life of prayer. This book proceeds from the priest's identity and ministry as a living image of Christ the bridegroom. The exploration of priestly spirituality presented in this section commences from the same nuptial vantage. As a consequence of this relationship, Pope Saint John Paul II writes, "In his spiritual life, therefore, [the priest] is called to live out Christ's spousal love toward the Church, his bride."[74] In addition to the insights from *Pastores Dabo Vobis*, the works of Thomas McGovern and Dermot Power offer helpful contributions to the examination of priestly spirituality. While the works of Galot and Toups explored above provide deeper insights into the sacramental character received in priestly ordination, the writings of McGovern and Power offer deeper understanding of priestly spirituality. These four authors enable a more comprehensive view of the facets of the spousal relationship between the priest and the church.

In the pivotal spousal paragraph of *Pastores Dabo Vobis* quoted above, Pope Saint John Paul II proposes several spiritual implications for the nuptial vision of priesthood. The spousal character of the priest's existence radiates in all aspects of his life. The priest is a witness to the spousal love of Christ and must "thus be capable of loving people with a heart which is new, generous and pure."[75] He lives and loves in a spirit of total dedication, genuine self-detachment, with the tenderness of a mother, and the protective jealousy reminiscent of Sinai.

Thomas McGovern views priestly spirituality through the lens of a spirituality of dedication.[76] Particularly fitting for a diocesan priest, he offers four characteristics: secularity, the exercise of ministry as a source of holiness, the unifying principle of pastoral charity, and unifying communion as the goal. Secularity refers to the dwelling of the priest in the community he serves. The priest shares a geographic location with his people; the bridegroom lives with the bride. He shops in the same stores, eats in the same restaurants, and visits the same coffee shops. He is not cloistered; the priest's tent is pitched among his people.[77] Through the exercise of his sacramental and pastoral duties, the priest grows in holiness. He experiences communion with the holy through prayer and through communion with the holy people. The exercise

---

74. John Paul II, *Pastores Dabo Vobis*, 22.
75. John Paul II, *Pastores Dabo Vobis*, 22.
76. McGovern, *Priestly Identity*, 132–33.
77. McGovern, *Priestly Identity*, 63–64; 130–32.

of priestly ministry is a gift of self and is motivated by pastoral charity. The priest offers service in love participating in Christ's own spousal love for the church. The communion of the church and the communion of individuals with the church is the primary goal of the priest's ministry.[78] The good of the community, analogous to the good of the spouses in marriage, is inherent in the mission and character of the priest.

Dermot Power posits six aspects of priestly spirituality.[79] Four of these focus on aspects of ministry: celebrating the eucharist, teaching and preaching, celebrating reconciliation, and intercessory prayer. The other two aspects concern the relationship of the priest to the people and the priest to Christ. Power notes as his fifth aspect the nearness of the priest to the people. This nearness is geographical and existential. Power writes, "The radical witness, therefore, of the priest of the parish rests in Christ's call to root priestly presence in the very fabric of the commonplace, everyday life of the people."[80] The final aspect regards the priest's intimacy with Christ: the priest remains a disciple. Burdened with the joys and challenges of pastoral ministry, the priest must return again and again to his filial identity as the foundation of his spousal identity and mission.[81]

Summary of Spirituality

The spousal countenance of priestly spirituality is summarized as motivation, location, and expression. Pastoral charity motivates the relationship and ministry of the priest and bears a spousal character. The relationship is lived in a common location, both geographically and existentially. Spousal love is expressed in the exercise of the priestly ministry, particularly in the celebration of the sacraments and other pastoral activities.

CONCLUSION

This chapter explored the spousal relationship between the priest and the Church. The overview of the ministerial priesthood provided the theological context from which the sacerdotal-ecclesial relationship emerges. The brief examination of Christ the Bridegroom and the church as bride provided the model for the relationship. Through the exploration of the royal

---

78. McGovern, *Priestly Identity*, 132–33.
79. Power, *Spiritual Theology of the Priesthood*, 113–31.
80. Power, *Spiritual Theology of the Priesthood*, 115.
81. Power, *Spiritual Theology of the Priesthood*, 130–31.

and ministerial priesthood, pastoral and ecclesial charity, fruitfulness, the sacramental bond, and spirituality, the various aspects of the spousal relationship seen in chapter 1 were applied to the nuptial union between the priest and the church. In the next chapter, the priest's ministry of preaching will be proposed and explored as an expression of spousal love.

Chapter 3

Preaching

An Expression of Spousal Love

DOES THE VOICE OF the Bridegroom echo in the church through the preaching of priests? It is the contention of this book that in the preaching act, the priest shares in the voice of the bridegroom just as he shares in the spousal relationship between Christ and the church. In chapter 1 several facets of the spousal relationship between husband and wife were examined.[1] Chapter 2 utilized those facets to explore the nuptial relationship between the priest and the church. This chapter proposes a nuptial vision for the priest's ministry of preaching. After a brief overview of nuptiality as a theological category, the basic characteristics of the proposed nuptial hermeneutic will be presented. This is followed by an application of the nuptial hermeneutic to the four constitutive parts of the preaching act as examined in the 1982 United States Bishop's document *Fulfilled in Your Hearing*.[2] These four parts are the assembly, the preacher, the homily, and the homiletical method. The organization provided by *Fulfilled in Your Hearing* offers an opportunity to explore the assembly and the preacher as relational partners in the preaching act.

---

1. These characteristics are asymmetrical reciprocity, love, the conjugal bond, the good of the spouses, fruitfulness, and spirituality.
2. Wallace, *Preaching in the Sunday Assembly*, 58–102.

For the purposes of this chapter, preaching refers to the homily given by a priest, usually the celebrant, during the celebration of the Eucharist. The nuptial vision of preaching presumes that the priest is a regular preacher in a stable community; this spousal model applies to resident, rather than itinerant, preachers. In a nuptial hermeneutic, preaching is an intimate activity rooted in the relationship between the preacher and the assembly who are mutually subordinate to each other as both preacher and assembly are subordinate unto the Lord (Eph 5:21).

The nuptial hermeneutic for preaching is grounded in nuptiality as a theological category. A brief exploration of the nuptial perspective in the broader context of theology provides a contextual foundation for the nuptial hermeneutic for preaching.

A NUPTIAL PERSPECTIVE

Angelo Cardinal Scola and Marc Cardinal Ouellet propose the nuptial mystery, or nuptiality, as a perspective for theological examination.[3] Ouellet provides an evaluation of nuptiality for sacramental theology while Scola offers an outline from the vantage of systematic theology. These perspectives enable applicability to the concept of nuptiality into other areas of theological investigation. The nuptial mystery is freed from the strict bonds of canon law, moral theology, and pastoral reflection to serve as a hermeneutical approach to the mysteries of the faith.[4]

Ouellet grounds his reflections in the category of covenant. The covenant, by which God invites the human community and the individual human person into relationship, is the fundamental category of expression in the Scriptures; the offering, renewing, and restoration of a covenant is the metanarrative.[5] Ouellet writes, "The covenant is God's institution of a unique bond between him and the people he has chosen: by virtue of this bond, God commits himself to his people, guaranteeing his protection and the fulfillment of his promises."[6] The covenant provides a unifying experience for the people and encompasses their identity, history, and future. The image of either the wedding feast or marriage is often used for this covenant and includes three stages of the experience of love: origin, exile,

---

3. Scola, *Nuptial Mystery*, 384–405. Ouellet, *Mystery and Sacrament of Love*, 112–23.
4. Scola, *Nuptial Mystery*, 385.
5. Ouellet, *Mystery and Sacrament of Love*, 113.
6. Ouellet, *Mystery and Sacrament of Love*, 113–14.

and rediscovery. These three stages are the pattern seen in the prophetic books of the Old Testament.[7]

Ouellet offers a second facet of the nuptial perspective: dramatic anthropology. The human person exists in a dialogical relationship which includes both the freedom of personal disclosure and the freedom of self-gift. A foundational element of this anthropological vision is the dual unity made possible by the complementarity of the male and the female. The human person is configured at the core of his or her being for communion and the primary way that this communion is sought and realized is the spousal union.[8]

A related aspect of nuptiality concerns the mystery of being. Being is envisioned as a gift. The meaning of being is unveiled in receptivity and in generosity. One receives the gift of the other and in response offers a gift of self. This mutual receiving and giving enables fruitfulness and self-realization.[9]

Cardinals Ouellet and Scola each present nuptiality from different, yet complementary, vantage points. Ouellet offers a nuptial perspective for sacramental theology rooted in covenant, dramatic anthropology, and the mystery of being. Scola, working in the broader discipline of systematic theology, grounds his proposal of nuptiality in anthropology, analogy, freedom, and language.

The human person as the *imago Dei* resides in the heart of the nuptial mystery. Each person is created in the image and likeness of God. The human capacity for relationship is of chief importance. The human person is created for communion with the other. The desire for *communio*, inscribed in human nature, is a fundamental anthropological category. Following the thinking of Pope Saint John Paul II, Scola notes that the *imago Dei* also resides in the unity of the man and the woman. The image of God is not exclusively, or even primarily, an individual; it is a communion of persons.[10]

A second facet of the human person as *imago Dei* concerns the human body. Historically, the image of God was thought to reside only in the mind or the soul. Scola notes, expounding on the thought of Pope Saint John Paul II, that the image of God includes the human body. The human body exists in sexual differentiation; sexual differentiation is part of what

---

7. Ouellet, *Mystery and Sacrament of Love*, 114–15. Ouellet provides as examples Hos 1:6; 2:7–15, 23; Jer 2:2–3; 31:33; Ezek 16; Isa 40–66.
8. Ouellet, *Mystery and Sacrament of Love*, 117–18.
9. Ouellet, *Mystery and Sacrament of Love*, 119–20.
10. Scola, *Nuptial Mystery*, 386–87.

it means to be human. The body is also understood as a sacrament of the whole person.[11]

These two insights about the human person, the capacity for communion and sexual differentiation, form the basis of this theological anthropology.[12] The two additional components of the nuptial mystery in Scola's tripartite schema are love and fruitfulness. Noting the foundational character of nuptiality, Scola writes, "Because it indicates an essential property of love, the nuptial mystery is present in every form of love, whether human or divine: in the man-woman relation, friendship, charity, the sacrament, the church, Jesus Christ, and the Trinity."[13] The ubiquitous presence of nuptiality in all manifestations of love allows the nuptial lens to be applied to all aspects of theology.

The nuptial perspective is grounded in an anthropological understanding. The human person is created as a gift and created for relationship. The covenant of marriage, which is a *communio personarum*, facilitates the growth of the spouses in freedom, maturity, and fruitfulness. This perspective can be applied through the use of analogy to the mysteries of faith.

Scola offers a caution in regard to the limits of analogy. On one extreme is a maximalist interpretation which equates the terms in an analogy. The other extreme denies that nuptiality is a proper vehicle for analogy. Scola opts for the middle path, a viewpoint which admits the benefits and limits of analogy.[14]

The final two aspects of the nuptial perspective, following anthropology and analogy, are freedom and the use of language. The exercise of freedom, by which a person chooses to make a gift of self, is called forth from the motive of love. Scola summarizes nuptial language stating that it "includes the one, the other, the unity of the two, the fruit of their union, and an indissolubility that brings into play the inevitable necessity of sacrifice as an essential part of love-desire."[15]

This brief analysis of the theological category of nuptiality offers a foundation for the nuptial hermeneutic for preaching. Building upon the theological category of nuptiality, the nuptial hermeneutic, or vision, of preaching will be explored in the next section.

---

11. Scola, *Nuptial Mystery*, 387–88.
12. Scola, *Nuptial Mystery*, 388.
13. Scola, *Nuptial Mystery*, 393.
14. Scola, *Nuptial Mystery*, 393–95.
15. Scola, *Nuptial Mystery*, 398.

THE NUPTIAL HERMENEUTIC

The nuptial vision, or hermeneutic, inspires and supports a relationship of *mutual kenotic vulnerability*. Typified by the spousal union between husband and wife and also seen in the relationship between the priest and the church, this relationship of mutual kenotic vulnerability exists by the mutual consent of the partners, involves a gift of self from both partners, and risks the harm or promotes the flourishing of both partners and their union.

The relationship of mutual kenotic vulnerability is realized and celebrated in the Eucharistic liturgy. As expressed in chapter 2, the celebration of the Eucharist manifests the union between Christ the Bridegroom and the bridal church. It is important to note that the entire celebration of the Eucharist, not just the consecration during the Eucharistic Prayer, is a nuptial expression. The liturgical setting is nuptial, and the liturgical space is the bridal chamber. Since the homily is an integral part of the Eucharistic liturgy, and the celebration of the Eucharist is a nuptial event, when the homily is preached by a priest who sacramentally represents Christ the bridegroom, the act of preaching is an expression of spousal love.

Preaching as an expression of spousal love is intentionally accomplished through the use of a nuptial hermeneutic. There are seven basic characteristics of a nuptial hermeneutic: fundamental equality, asymmetrical or relational reciprocity, motivated by love, open to fruitfulness, a stable relationship, supportive spirituality, and service to *koinonia*.

The fundamental equality of the partners is the foundational characteristic of the nuptial hermeneutic. This equality is rooted in creation and baptism. The individual members of the assembly, the assembly gathered as a body for worship, and the priest are each an *imago Dei*. Before any distinction of roles, rank, or ministry, each member of the community gathered for worship is a disciple. Expressing this fundamental equality, the community is constituted as a *we*.

At the same time, the community gathered for worship is constituted by *you and me*. The second characteristic of the nuptial hermeneutic is asymmetrical or relational reciprocity. The asymmetrical reciprocity of male and female in the marital relationship is analogously manifest in the priest-church relationship through the two participations in the one priesthood of Christ. The baptized members of the assembly share in the royal priesthood and the ordained priests share in the ministerial priesthood. These two participations are ordered to each other. The assembly and the priest share an ontological complementarity; they are made for relationship with each other.

The third characteristic is that the relationship between the assembly and the priest is motivated by love. As explored in chapter 2, pastoral charity describes the love by which the priest loves and serves the church. On the part of the priest, pastoral charity motivates the relationship. On the part of the baptized, ecclesial charity describes the love by which the faithful receive and respond to pastoral charity. As love is the animating principle of the spousal relationship between husband and wife, so too love motivates the relationship between the preacher and the assembly.

The first three characteristics of the nuptial hermeneutic include equality, reciprocity, and love; these are the necessary conditions for the relationship to exist and constitute the essence of the relationship. The following two characteristics are concerned with maintaining the relationship.

The fourth characteristic of the nuptial hermeneutic is that the preaching occurs in a stable relationship. In the marital union, this stability is referred to as permanence. The preaching relationship is not permanent. Priests are transferred and the faithful move. However, both the priest and the baptized possess an indelible sacramental character which bonds them to a permanent relationship to Christ and to the church. In a general sense, the relationship is permanent; in a temporal sense, it is not. The relationship between the priest and the community is usually stable, either by term or indefinite appointment. The implication for preaching is that time is needed to build a relationship in which loving and challenging words can be spoken and accepted. A stable relationship is also needed for the mutual growth of the preacher and the assembly. Spousal preaching flourishes in an environment where tomorrow can be reasonably presumed, though of course not guaranteed.

The fifth characteristic of the nuptial vision of preaching is a supportive spirituality. The aspects of this spirituality are found at the intersection of the spirituality of marriage explored in chapter 1 and the spirituality of the priesthood examined in chapter 2. A spirituality rooted in the nuptial hermeneutic builds communion through affirmation of identity, loving attention, patient expectation, and local dedication.

These characteristics of a stable relationship and supportive spirituality are sustaining components of the nuptial hermeneutic and union. Building on the foundational characteristics of equality, asymmetrical or relational reciprocity, and love, stability and spirituality maintain and support the relationship enabling fruitfulness and communal flourishing.

The nuptial vision is open to fruitfulness. This sixth characteristic recognizes the generative potential and power of the relationship. In the spousal union between husband and wife, fruitfulness is manifest in children, social action, growth in holiness, and evangelical witness. As noted in chapter 2, fruitfulness in the relationship between the priest and the church is doxological, spiritual, vocational, and homiletical. Emphasis in this chapter is on homiletical fruitfulness. The nuptial hermeneutic affirms the dignity of the assembly and the priest as equal relational partners, reverences the procreative potential of this union, and seeks to carefully overcome obstacles to receptivity and fruitfulness in the preacher and the assembly.

The seventh and final characteristic of the nuptial hermeneutic is service to *koinonia*. This term, which can analogously correspond to the good of the spouses, expresses a relationship. *Koinonia* refers to interdependence, fellowship, community, association, and communion.[16] In his biography of Paul, N. T. Wright defines *koinonia* as the sharing of goods, resources, and the deep and interpersonal sharing of life. He writes, "When we wonder what most strongly motivated Paul, we must put at the center the fact that at a deeply human level he was sustained and nourished by what he came to call *koinonia*."[17] The deep interpersonal relationship expressed by the term *koinonia* in which resources, affection, and lives are shared is sought, supported, and actualized through the nuptial hermeneutic.

The seven characteristics of the nuptial vision illuminate the foundation, sustaining support, and fruitful extension of the spousal relationship. These characteristics will be utilized to explore the implications of the nuptial hermeneutic and its application on the assembly, the preacher, the homily, and homiletical method.

THE ASSEMBLY

The assembly is the preacher's relational partner in the preaching act; the assembly is the bride.[18] The nuptial hermeneutic influences the preacher's approach to, engagement with, and expectation of the assembly. In this section, the theological significance of the assembly as bride will be reviewed and the homiletical disciplines of congregational exegesis, reader or listener response criticism, and the womanist perspective will be explored.

In the nuptial vision of preaching, the preacher approaches the assembly recognizing that "she is his equal and an heir to the life of grace."[19] Viewed as an equal and as a relational partner, the assembly is the recipient

---

16. Mahohoma, "Difficult Texts: *Koinonia*, Acts 2.42," 364–66.

17. Wright, *Paul: A Biography*, 190.

18. For the purposes of this theological examination, the preacher is not part of the assembly.

19. *Order for Celebrating Matrimony*, First Nuptial Blessing.

of the preacher's love, devotion, affection, and work. The bridal assembly enjoys the freedom to accept or reject the gift of preaching offered by the preacher and therefore possesses a determining disposition in regard to the fruitfulness of preaching. The active receptivity of the bridal assembly is initiated and strengthened through a supportive spirituality in a stable pastoral relationship. In the nuptial vision of preaching, the preacher approaches the assembly with a spirit of reverence, a willingness to sacrifice and suffer, a desire to repair and restore, and with a view to resurrection and eternal life. The preacher approaches the bridal assembly with the same characteristics as the marital spirituality of tenderness examined in chapter 1. The tender approach of the preacher recognizes the dignity of the assembly, respects the relational reciprocity, honors the fruitful potential, and supports the stability of the union between the preacher and the assembly.

The nuptial hermeneutic for preaching impacts how the preacher engages the assembly. Approached with tenderness, the preacher appreciates the complexities and the unique identity of a bridal assembly. The brief theological analysis explored above notes the general characteristics of every assembly of the baptized. The section on the preacher's engagement examines the various aspects of a particular assembly. Congregational exegesis, reader or listener response criticism, and the womanist perspective assist in this examination. When viewed through the lens of the nuptial hermeneutic, these three homiletical disciplines transpose into the nuptial categories of knowing the bride, honoring the bride, and caring for the bride.

Knowing the Bride

The first of the three nuptial categories is knowing the bride. The practice of congregational exegesis seeks to carefully examine the nature, complexity, and qualities of the assembly. In her book, *Preaching as Local Theology and Folk Art*, Leonora Tubbs Tisdale proposes an interdisciplinary method for careful congregational exegesis.[20] Her approach begins with the notion that a congregation can be examined as an anthropological subculture. In this method, the preacher utilizes the discipline of ethnography which identifies and analyzes important symbols in the community.[21] The preacher is a participant-observer within the congregational subculture, meaning that the preacher shares in the life and activities of the community.[22]

20. Tisdale, *Preaching as Local Theology*, 56–77.
21. Tisdale, *Preaching as Local Theology*, 58–62.
22. For further explanation of the participant-observer, see Tisdale, *Preaching as Local Theology*, 60. In the theological analysis above, the preacher and assembly are

The first step of exegesis in this model seeks the identification and investigation of symbols in the culture. Tisdale proposes five guidelines for this process. The first is to determine the "texts" that hold significant symbolic value in the community. Artifacts, written documents, often repeated stories, observances, controversies, and celebrations are examples of such texts. The second guideline is to investigate the multiple forms in which the congregational texts appear. These include hymnody, ritual, historical markers, liturgical vessels and vestments and architecture. The third and fourth of Tisdale's guidelines encourage diligence in exegesis when contradictory or dissonant symbols are uncovered or the depth of complexity within congregational symbols appear. The last guideline for identification and investigation of symbols in a culture recommends attention to those texts which indicate social change, conflict and resolution, and liminal events in the life of the community.[23] These five guidelines enable the preacher to discover the textual symbols which the bridal assembly values. The following paragraphs provide an analysis of Tisdale's application of these guidelines for a symbolic exegesis of the congregation.

Table 3.1 Symbols for Congregational Exegesis[24]

Symbol Name	Examples	What the Symbol Reveals
	Foundational Symbols	
Stories and Interviews	Stories told within and outside the congregation, interviews with parishioners	Congregational identity, social change, names of leaders/controversies
Archival Materials	Charter documents, minutes from councils, photo directories, sacramental records	Provides official data confirming or contradicting presentation in stories and interviews

---

relational partners. In an ethnographic analysis, the preacher is a participant-observer essentially dwelling within the assembly. In both cases, the preacher is related to the assembly and remains distinct from it. The preacher is both an insider and an outsider to the community.

23. Tisdale, *Preaching as Local Theology*, 61–64.

24. Sourced from Tisdale, *Preaching as Local Theology*, 64–77. This table was created by me.

Demographics	Statistics of cultural, ethnic, racial, economic, social class, age, educational makeup of congregation	Current picture of the congregation and indications of change when compared with previous demographics
	Symbols of Celebration	
Architecture and Visual Arts	Church buildings, artwork, liturgical vessels/vestments	Where the community celebrates
Rituals	Baptisms, weddings, funerals, first communion, confirmations	How the community celebrates
Events and Activities	Festivals, picnics, educational programs, community events	What the community celebrates
People	Congregational leaders, heroes, those who are honored and those who are neglected or not mentioned	Whom the community celebrates

To apply the five guidelines Leonora Tubbs Tisdale proposes identification and investigation of symbols in a culture, Tisdale enumerates seven symbols for congregational exegesis.[25] The first of these symbols focuses on interviews and stories provided by members of the congregation. These can offer both eyewitness testimony and hearsay regarding the history and life of the congregation. A second symbol is archival materials. These include historical documents, financial and sacramental records, minutes from councils and committees, official reports, and parish histories. The third symbol is a demographic analysis. This provides a current picture of the makeup of the congregation utilizing several characteristics such as "sex, race, ethnicity, social class, educational level, power or prestige."[26] Of particular importance is the change in congregational demographics narrated by stories and interviews and documented by archival materials. These first three symbols provide the foundations of congregational exegesis while the remaining four symbols can be viewed through the window of celebration.[27]

The four symbols of celebration proposed by Tisdale include visual arts and architecture, rituals, activities and events, and the people who

---

25. Tisdale, *Preaching as Local Theology*, 64–77.
26. Tisdale, *Preaching as Local Theology*, 70.
27. The window of celebration in regard to these four symbols is my analysis.

are honored or whose names and voices are avoided in the community.[28] Where the community celebrates, how they celebrate, what they celebrate, and whom they celebrate are illuminated through these four congregational symbols. The celebratory window allows the history, contemporary reality, and future hopes of the congregation to be recognized and examined.

In addition to the symbolic analysis, Tisdale notes the importance of a theological analysis of the congregation. She proposes six broad theological categories to facilitate this analysis: view of God, view of humanity, view of nature, view of time, view of the church, view of Christian mission, and the interrelationships of the other categories.[29]

The congregational view of God includes the theological disciplines of theology, Christology, and pneumatology. Primarily, the congregational vantage is demonstrated on the continuum between the imminence and transcendence of God. These views are exemplified in hymnody, ritual, celebration, and popular piety. Additionally, these views impact the recognition of miracles, the role of intercessory prayer, and the relationship between justice and mercy.[30]

The theological anthropology of the congregation reflects its understanding of the human person. This is demonstrated through the principle descriptions of identity. For example, in the congregational analysis is a person primarily a beloved child of God or a sinner in need of redemption? While both descriptions are theologically accurate, the more prominent description used within the congregation reflects its understanding and impacts its ministry.[31]

The congregational views on creation and time reflect its relationship to nature and history. If the world is viewed as something passing away and the consummation of history more proximate, then care for creation and efforts to create a more just society will be lower priorities. On the other hand, if the goodness of creation is valued and the presence of the reign of God can be experienced in some manner now, then both ecological and social justice find space in the ministry of the congregation.[32]

Ecclesiology and mission concern the internal and external relationships of the community. The understanding of the church can be seen in the metaphors employed by the congregation. Body, bride, communion, sacrament, pilgrim people, sanctuary, hospital, and many others are

---

28. Tisdale, *Preaching as Local Theology*, 71–77.
29. Tisdale, *Preaching as Local Theology*, 80–86.
30. Tisdale, *Preaching as Local Theology*, 80–81.
31. Tisdale, *Preaching as Local Theology*, 80–81.
32. Tisdale, *Preaching as Local Theology*, 81.

metaphorical understandings that impact the understanding of mission.[33] The understanding of mission is often manifest in the programs and the budget of the community.

These various theological viewpoints interrelate to form the theological identity of the congregation. In the nuptial vision, these reflect the deeply held beliefs and convictions of the bride and must be respected and honored even though they may be challenged by the preaching of the bridegroom.

The discipline of congregational exegesis presented by Leonora Tubbs Tisdale offers a method for the symbolic and theological analysis of the congregation. Utilizing these counsels provides the nuptial hermeneutic with an effective and reverent way of knowing the bridal assembly. Knowing the complexity of the assembly, the bride, the bridegroom preacher is better equipped to show her honor.

Honoring the Bride

The second of the three nuptial categories is honoring the bride. When the words of the homily are preached, the preacher surrenders the interpretation of those words to the listeners. The words do not belong exclusively to preacher anymore. Sarah Jane Smith notes that "the sermon comes into existence when it is preached and interpreted through the hearing of its message."[34] The realization of a homily or sermon is only fulfilled in the hearing of the assembly. Smith continues, "Because listeners shape the hearing of the sermon in significant ways, they are, in effect, the sermon's co-creators."[35]

The discipline regarding reader or listener-response criticism provides the nuptial hermeneutic with a method to honor the receptivity of the bride. Sarah Jane Smith offers five characteristics of listener-response [criticism] and five homiletical tools which correspond to these characteristics.[36] Through the use of these five characteristics and the corresponding homiletical tools, the preacher honors the dignity of the bridal assembly as a receptive relational partner in the preaching act.

The first characteristic of listener-response criticism is that hearing and response are shaped by interpretive communities which are diverse in any community. Interpretive communities share common social, political, theological, cultural, and philosophical views. Usually, there are multiple

---

33. Tisdale, *Preaching as Local Theology*, 83–84.
34. Smith, "Reader/Listener Response," 161.
35. Smith, "Reader/Listener Response," 161
36. Smith, "Reader/Listener Response," 161–63.

interpretive communities within an assembly and individuals may belong to several of them at once. Smith proposes the homiletical tool of identification where the preacher employs various points of view and the interpretive communities within the assembly can recognize their communal and philosophical interaction with the sermon. This first characteristic notes that interpretation is a communal activity.

The second characteristic of listener-response criticism is that interpretation is a reflection of identity. Interpretation is personal. Everything that is presented is received through the kaleidoscope of personal experiences. Responding to this personal interpretative reality, Smith suggests the homiletical tool of connection. The use of polyvalent material, that which allows multiple meanings, invites the individuals within the assembly to recognize their own experiences within the sermon. As the first characteristic concerns the communal, that is public, nature of interpretation, the second characteristic focuses on conscious or subconscious activity of the individual.

The third characteristic is, "Listeners interact with the framework of sermon structure and content to make meaning."[37] The structural form of the sermon and the content impacts how the sermon is received by the listeners. Smith notes the homiletical tool of anticipation in which the preacher posits an implied listener in homiletical preparation. Through the use of anticipation, the sermon is constructed with a particular assembly in mind. This third principle of listener-response criticism concerns the preacher as the interpreter of the assembly and the interpreter of the message proclaimed.

The fourth characteristic is that new understandings are made possible by homiletical listening. Smith suggests the homiletical tool of reinterpretation in which the interplay of ideas leads to new understandings. She notes three ways that encourage listener reinterpretation: wandering viewpoints, blanks, and negations. Wandering viewpoints take a past experience and infuse it with a new perspective for interpretation. A new perspective leads to renewed understanding; it offers a new way to look at old events or concepts. Blanks are places where only the essential details or structure are given so that the listeners can form their own conclusions. Blanks are questions, options, proposals, and phrases that "leave open places within the sermon and give the listener an opportunity to connect with the message, making it personal."[38] Negations present a familiar idea, concept, or situation and then cancels it to offer a new understanding. Negations can be discomforting for the assembly because they require a change in familiar

---

37. Smith, "Reader/Listener Response," 162.
38. Smith, "Reader/Listener Response," 163.

thinking. While often very effective, negations need to be utilized with great care. This fourth principle presents one of the fruits of listener-response criticism: new understandings and insights are conceived through homiletical listening.

The fifth and final characteristic is that homiletical listening enables transformation. Transformation is also the homiletical tool noted by Smith. This concerns the response of the listeners; it is an extended fruit from new understandings. New ways of response and new visions of discipleship are presented as possibilities to the listeners. Transformation occurs from the dialogue between the preacher and the listener in the sermon. The relationship between the preacher and the listeners is most open to transformation when the members of the assembly are not commanded, but invited.[39]

The discipline of listener-response criticism offers the nuptial hermeneutic a method to honor the receptivity of the bridal assembly. By attending to the various interpretive communities, personal identities, homiletical structures, and new understanding, the relationship between the preacher and the assembly is rendered transformative and fruitful, expressing care for the bride.

Knowing the bride and honoring the bride are critical dimensions of the spousal relationship. In the next section, a third nuptial category, caring for the bride, will be explored.

Caring for the Bride

While the discipline of congregational exegesis respects the complexity of the community and the reader- or listener-response criticism honors receptivity, the insights of womanist theological reflection enables the preacher to attend to the woundedness in the community. Knowing, naming, and attending to the communal and individual wounds in the congregation reflects a deep level of intimacy between the preacher and the community. Attention to the woundedness must be approached gently and carefully—this is delicate work. The womanist perspective, while rooted in the experience of African American women, analogously offers a methodological approach for attending to the woundedness in all and each of the men and women in the community: it counsels a way to care for the bride.

In her work, *God in Her Midst: Preaching Healing to Wounded Women*, Elaine M. Flake enumerates six interpretive methods which can be effective in ministry to the wounded.[40] Utilizing the six interpretive practices: one

39. Smith, "Reader/Listener Response," 163.
40. Flake, *God in Her Midst*, 12–18.

affirms, shows sensitivity, honors tradition, liberates, presents Jesus as an advocate, and acknowledges history.

The first interpretive methodology encouraged by Flake is to affirm. In the womanist context, affirmation involves highlighting the positive roles that women, and particularly women of color, play in the scriptural texts and in history. In the congregational context, the interpretive method of affirmation seeks those who are at the margins: those who experience or perceive neglect, isolation, exclusion, or rejection from the regular ministry and preaching in the community.[41] Through the interpretive method of affirmation, the preacher notices the unnoticed.[42] The preacher recognizes human and Christian dignity before proclaiming the healing challenge of the gospel. Flake notes, "An affirming word is a healing word."[43] The methodological practice of affirmation provides the foundation for the subsequent interpretive methods.

Building upon the foundation of affirmation, the second interpretive practice proposed by Flake is to show sensitivity. Sensitivity recognizes the breadth of circumstances that influence belief and behavior. The lives of individuals and communities are larger stories than the brief events recounted in a scriptural text or a homiletical illustration. Sensitivity requires attention to texts, images, anecdotes, and language which might further wound the wounded. Through the practice of showing sensitivity, the preacher recognizes and attends to the "full spectrum of life circumstances," present in the community.[44]

The first two methodological practices of affirming and showing sensitivity support the third interpretive practice whereby the preacher honors tradition. From the womanist perspective, Flake cautions that "care must be taken that the emergent preaching is not stripped of traditional elements that are a source of comfort and liberation for African American women."[45] In the congregational context, to honor the tradition is to recognize and celebrate the Bethanys, Galilees, and Gileads, those places both physical and existential which bring comfort in the personal and communal history. Honoring the tradition requires attention to the sacred texts—scriptural, liturgical, musical, and homiletical—which support and inspire the community. While the practice of showing sensitivity

---

41. Flake, *God in Her Midst*, 13–14.

42. Just as Jesus, in the Gospel of Luke, often focuses on the poor, widows, and the marginalized.

43. Flake, *God in Her Midst*, 14.

44. Flake, *God in Her Midst*, 14.

45. Flake, *God in Her Midst*, 15.

indicates those things that the preacher desires to avoid, the practice of honoring the tradition reveals those things that the preacher would want to highlight.

The fourth interpretive practice concerns liberation—the proclamation of the gospel brings freedom.[46] To proclaim liberation is to first understand the sources of bondage and oppression experienced within the community. While the practice of affirmation announces dignity and the practices of showing sensitivity and honoring the tradition respect history, the interpretive practice of liberation proclaims a future, and specifically a future full of hope (Jer 29:11–14a). Through the interpretive method of liberation, the preacher declares the freeing and healing power of God against the forces of oppression and bondage.[47]

The fifth interpretive method presents Jesus as the advocate for the wounded. In the womanist context, this refers to the multiple ways Jesus affirms the dignity of women, especially against the cultural and religious norms.[48] In the congregational context, every gospel pericope which shows Jesus attending to the sick, poor, grieving, isolated or rejected is an opportunity to proclaim Jesus as an advocate for the wounded. The entire earthly ministry of Jesus manifests his advocacy for the wounded. Through this interpretive method, the preacher presents the agent of affirmation, sensitivity, honor, and liberation to the community.[49]

The sixth and final interpretive practice proposed by Elaine Flake is to acknowledge African ancestry. In the womanist context, this is realized by affirming and celebrating the accounts of women of color in the scriptures.[50] In the congregational context, which seeks to honor persons of every culture, heritage, race, and era, this concerns scriptural accounts and the lives of the holy people of God which affirm the dignity and liberation of the wounded. This interpretive principle offers encouragement for those who are suffering. Through the application of this interpretive principle, the preacher offers the community the image of one who was wounded and has been healed—a concrete example that liberation and healing are possible.

---

46. For example, Luke 4:16–30.
47. Flake, *God in Her Midst*, 16.
48. Luke is sometimes referred to as the Gospel of Women for precisely this reason.
49. Flake, *God in Her Midst*, 17.
50. Flake, *God in Her Midst*, 17–18.

Table 3.2 Interpretive Principles[51]

Interpretive Practice	Womanist Context	Congregational/ Nuptial Context	Effect
Affirm	Highlights positive roles that women, particularly women of color, play in scriptural texts and in history	Seeks the marginalized: who experience or perceive exclusion or rejection from the regular ministry and preaching in the community	Recognizes human and Christian dignity; Foundational for the other five interpretive practices
Show Sensitivity	Recognizes the breadth of circumstances that influence belief and behavior	Recognizes the breadth of circumstances that influence belief and behavior	Attends to the many circumstances of life, particularly with images and language to avoid
Honor Tradition	Recognizes traditional/historical sources of comfort and liberation for African American women	Recognizes traditional/historical sources of comfort and liberation for members of the assembly	Indicates those traditional events/themes/places to be highlighted and celebrated
Liberate	Recognizes sources of bondage and oppression and proclaims future of freedom and hope	Recognizes sources of bondage and oppression and proclaims future of freedom and hope	Declares freedom and healing by God's power
Present Jesus as an Advocate for Women	Presents ways Jesus affirms the dignity of women	Presents ways Jesus affirms dignity of/ advocates for the wounded	Proclaims Jesus as agent of healing and liberation
Acknowledge African Ancestry	Affirms/ celebrates the accounts of women of color in the scriptures	Honors persons of every culture, heritage, race, and era as models	Offers image of one wounded and then healed

51. *Source*: Flake, *God in Her Midst*, 12–18. This table was created by me.

The six interpretive methods from the womanist perspective presented by Elaine Flake offer the nuptial hermeneutic a strategy to care for the bride. Through the practice of affirmation, the preacher recognizes the dignity of the assembly and the individuals who are part of that assembly. By showing sensitivity and honoring the tradition, the preacher respects the present and the past of the community. The interpretive method of liberation offers the promise of healing, freedom, and hope. Presenting Jesus as the advocate for the wounded announces the agent of healing; acknowledging ancestry offers a concrete example of care for the wounded and healing for the hurting. Through the use of these interpretive practices, the notion of caring for the bride is sure to be preserved from descending into offensive patronizing; it will demonstrate the love of the preacher for the bridal assembly by respecting her dignity and equality while gently attending to her wounds.

Summary of the Assembly

In the nuptial vision of preaching, the assembly is the bride. Loved, honored, attended to, and respected, the assembly is the bridegroom preacher's relational partner. The homiletical disciplines of congregational exegesis, reader or listener response criticism, and insights from the womanist perspective honor the complexity, receptivity, and woundedness of the bridal assembly. These three disciplines provide the nuptial hermeneutic and the bridegroom preacher with ways to know, honor, and care for the bride.

The spousal relationship exists between two equal partners: the bride and the bridegroom. Analogously, in the nuptial preaching relationship, these partners are the bridal assembly and the bridegroom preacher. Having explored the identity and complexity of the bride, the next section examines the preacher as bridegroom.

THE PREACHER

The preacher is the bridegroom in the nuptial hermeneutic. Following the examination of the assembly, the implications of the nuptial hermeneutic and its application on the preacher will be explored in this section. He is the bridegroom preacher and is ontologically ordered for relationship with the bride. He loves, knows, honors, and attends to the bridal assembly offering her a complete gift of self in a stable relationship which is open to multiform fruitfulness and is enhanced through a supportive spirituality. The nuptial vision impacts the understanding of the preacher's identity, authority, and motivation.

Identity

The preacher discovers his identity in relationship. As a ministerial priest, he lives in a specific relationship with the Father, with Christ, with the Holy Spirit, and with the church. Christ shares with the ministerial priest his own relationship with the church as Bridegroom. The spousal relationship between the priest and the church that was explored in chapter 2 is rooted in the fundamental equality of all disciples, the relational reciprocity between the royal and ministerial participations in the priesthood of Christ, and the love that animates the relationship. A supportive spirituality sustains this stable relationship and is open to fruitfulness. Through this spousal union, both the priest and the members of the assembly grow in faith, virtue, and holiness. In the nuptial hermeneutic, the preacher is the bridegroom.

The identity of the bridegroom preacher can be fittingly explored using the three meanings of the body proposed by Pope Saint John Paul II which were examined in chapter 1. As the three meanings of the body are filial, spousal, and parental, analogously the three dimensions of the bridegroom preacher's identity are receptive, unitive, and generative. The receptive dimension indicates that the bridegroom receives the foundation of his identity from another: from God and the church. His identity as a child of God is ontologically and temporally prior to his mission and identity as a bridegroom and preacher. The receptive dimension reflects the bridegroom preacher's fundamental equality with the members of the assembly. He is, with each of them, a disciple and a hearer of the Word. The preacher is first a listener. Whenever the receptive dimension of the bridegroom preacher's identity is neglected or ignored, the capacity for the unitive dimension is compromised. Receptive listening, to God in the scriptures, to the church in her teaching, and to the multiform voice of the bridal assembly, is not simply a task for the preacher to accomplish—it is foundational for his identity. The receptive dimension grounds the identity of the bridegroom preacher.

The unitive dimension builds upon the receptive. Before the preacher can speak, he must listen. By ordination to the ministerial priesthood, the bridegroom preacher is ordered at the core of his being to relationship with the bridal assembly. The unitive dimension manifests the relational reciprocity between the royal and ministerial participations in the priesthood of Christ. The priest cannot find his identity except by relationship to the Church and her members. In a sense, the unitive dimension is a deepening of the receptive dimension—the bridegroom receives the gift of the bride. The unitive relationship involves mutual giving and receiving as an essential characteristic. The bridegroom preacher makes a gift of self in kenotic vulnerability, offering to the bridal assembly the totality of his person, mission, and message as an act of love. Surrounding this gift of self, the bridegroom preacher receives the gift of the bridal assembly's presence, kenotic vulnerability, and response of love. When either partner in this relationship withholds the gift of self in presence, vulnerability, or love, the unitive dimension is damaged or possibly prevented. The receptive dimension requires openness and vulnerability before God and the universal church. The unitive dimension necessitates vulnerability and openness to the concrete, incarnate, and particular community of the parish church. The unitive dimension, which builds upon the receptive and makes possible the generative dimension, requires the loving trust of both partners.

The generative dimension flows from the receptive and unitive dimensions. The gift of identity received in the foundational dimension and shared in the unitive dimension is extended in the generative dimension. The strengthening of the bond between the bridegroom preacher and the bridal assembly along with the multiple fruits of that bond manifest the generative dimension. To be fruitful is a function of identity. The generative dimension is a constitutive part that defines who the bridegroom preacher is, and not simply part of what he does.

These three dimensions are at the heart of the nuptial hermeneutic for preaching. Listening, sharing, and extending are manifestations of the preacher's identity. Failure to engage these dimensions is not a neglect of the preacher's mission; they reflect a betrayal of who the preacher is.

The nuptial hermeneutic impacts the understanding of the preacher's identity. The next section explores the authority of the preacher.

Authority

The authority of the preacher flows from configuration to Christ and relationship to the church: it is filial, official, and relational. The nuptial hermeneutic values relational authority most. Reflection on these three dimensions offers the bridegroom preacher insights into the nature and exercise of authority in his relationship to the bridal assembly.

The preacher is a child of God and a hearer of the word. Expressive of the fundamental equality between the preacher and the assembly, the foundational authority is that of a listener. The preacher is one who has heard and who still hears the proclamation of the good news. When all liturgical ministries are present and active, the celebrant hears the scriptures proclaimed with the members of the assembly; he joins the assembly to receive the gift of the word. As Charles Rice notes, "For the preacher, no less than for the congregation, the sermon begins in hearing the biblical language."[52] The preacher always remains a disciple; his authority to preach is grounded first in his ability to listen. Filial authority is conferred by baptism.

Only one who shares in the royal priesthood of the baptized can be called to share in the ministerial priesthood of the ordained. Only listeners can be authentically called to be preachers. Building upon the filial authority as a listener, the priest receives through ordination and juridical appointment an official authority to preach. As the Code of Canon Law states, "The people of God are first united through the word of the living God, and are fully entitled to seek this word from their priests. For this reason sacred ministers are to consider the office of preaching as of great importance, since proclaiming the Gospel of God to all is among their principal duties."[53] The official authority of the preacher is given in response to a right of the faithful. The people of God are entitled to preaching. Priests, especially those who exercise pastoral care, have a responsibility and are qualified by education, ordination, and appointment to satisfy this right. The official authority of the preacher is an authority of service. This authority is conferred by the Bishop in ordination and by juridical appointment to a particular place or mission.

The third dimension of authority is relational authority. It is conferred on the preacher by the community without rite or ceremony. John S. McClure summarizes the work of many homileticians stating that relational authority "comes from developing good pastoral and personal relationships and fostering a sense of the human quest for authenticity and shared values so that listeners will trust what the preacher says."[54] The relational dimension of authority builds upon both filial and official authority and develops over time. Relational authority cannot be rushed. There is a necessary season for gestation. When the community offers the gift of relational authority to the preacher in the liturgy, it is a fruit of the relationship between the priest and members of the assembly outside of the liturgy. It is a manifestation of ecclesial charity and an act of vulnerability on the part of the royal priesthood in response to the pastoral charity and vulnerability of the ministerial priest. Relational authority exists within the relationship of mutual kenotic vulnerability. It enables fruitfulness, strengthens the bond, and serves the *koinonia*. While there is no liturgical or sacramental rite for conferring relational authority, there is a linguistic ritual. Filial and official

---

52. Rice, "Authority of the Preacher," 220.
53. *Code of Canon Law*, 762.
54. McClure, *Preaching Words*, 8.

authority is designated with an article: "the" priest. Relational authority is revealed with a possessive pronoun: "our" or "my" priest.

The preacher possesses authority in virtue of baptism, ordination, and appointment, and by the gift of the community. These three dimensions build upon the other with the filial being foundational and the relational as fruitful. The nuptial hermeneutic employs all three aspects of authority carefully attending to the exercise of the authority of the listener and the authority of office as the gift of relational authority is awaited in joyful hope.

The two preceding sections addressed the preacher's identity and the authority of the preacher as it relates to the nuptial hermeneutic. The next section will explore the understanding of the preacher's motivation.

Motivation

On June 15, 1917, Pope Benedict XV issued the second encyclical of his pontificate. Entitled *Humani Generis Redemptionem* "On Preaching the Word of God," this is the most recent papal document at the level of an encyclical or apostolic exhortation specifically focused on preaching. Each of the popes have addressed preaching in one way or another in their writings, but this was the most recent document from a pope specifically focused on preaching.[55] In this encyclical, he presents three causes of poor preaching: poor selection in preachers, defective intention of preachers, and poor performance by preachers. Concerning the intention of preachers, Pope Benedict XV writes that preachers "ought to have the same purpose in discharging their office that Christ had in conferring it on them."[56] Preachers testify to the truth so that their hearers may have life (John 10:10). The Holy Father warns against preachers who seek applause or seek to acquire fame or other earthly benefits. Of these preachers he says, "They seem to have only one aim, to please their hearers and curry favor with those whom St. Paul describes as 'having itching ears.'"[57] For Pope Benedict XV, clarifying the intention or motivation of preachers is a critical component for the renewal of preaching.[58]

In the nuptial hermeneutic, preaching is motivated by love. Saint John Chrysostom commented on the love of the preacher for the community in his thirteenth homily on Saint Paul's Second Letter to the Corinthians. His analysis of Saint Paul's love for his communities merits an extended quotation.

55. See Roberts, "From Benedict to Francis," para. 1.
56. Benedict XV, *Humani Generis Redemptionem*, 9.
57. Benedict XV, *Humani Generis Redemptionem*, 10.
58. For additional perspective see Francis, *Evangelii Gaudium*, chapter 3, 135–75.

Our heart is enlarged. For as heat makes things expand, so it is the work of love to expand the heart, for its power is to heat and make fervent. It is this that opened Paul's lips and enlarged his heart. *For I do not love only in words*; he means, *but my loving heart too is in unison with my words; and so I speak with confidence, without restraint or reserve.* There was nothing more capacious than the heart of Paul, for he loved all the faithful with as intimate a love as any lover could have for a loved one, his love not being divided and lessened but remaining whole and entire for each of them. And what marvel is it that his love for the faithful was such, since his heart embraced the unbelievers, too, throughout the whole world?

So he did not just say, "I love you," but with greater emphasis: *Our mouth is open, our heart is enlarged*; we hold you all in it, and not only that, but with room for you to move freely. For those who are loved enter fearlessly into the heart of their lover. And therefore he says: *You are not constrained because of us, but you are constrained in your own affections.* See how this reproach is tempered with much forbearance, as is the way with those who love much. For he did not say: *You do not love me, but you do not love me in the same measure*; for he did not want to charge them more harshly.

Indeed one may see with what a wonderful love for the faithful he is always inflamed, as one finds proof of it in all his writings. To the Romans he says: *I desire to see you, and I have often planned to come to you, and if by any means at last I may succeed in reaching you.* To the Galatians he says: *My little children, with whom I am again in labor;* to the Ephesians: *For this reason I bend my knees on your behalf;* and to the Thessalonians: *What is my hope and my crown of glory? Is it not yourselves?* For he used to say that he carried them about in his heart and in his chains.

Again he writes to the Colossians: *I want you to know how greatly I strive for you and for all who have not seen my face;* and to the Thessalonians: *Like a nurse taking care of her children, being desirous of you, we were ready to share with you not only the Gospel but also our own selves.* So too he says: *You are not restricted by us.* And so Paul does not merely say that he loves them but also that they love him, so that in this way he may draw them to him. Indeed, to the Corinthians he bears witness of this love when he says: *Titus came, telling us of your longing, your mourning, your zeal for me.*[59]

---

59. Saint John Chrysostom, *Homily 13 on 2nd Corinthians*, This section is taken from the Liturgy of the Hours, Second Reading, Saturday of the 16th Week in Ordinary Time.

Love motivates preaching. This does not exclude the desires to evangelize, catechize, exhort, encourage, or testify: love unifies them. As explored in chapter 2, pastoral charity is that love which is proper to the ministerial priesthood. It motivates and vivifies all actions in ministry. Rooted in Christ's spousal and sacrificial love for the church, pastoral charity animates a gift of self by the priest to the church in her universal, particular, and parochial manifestations.[60] The nuptial hermeneutic envisions preaching as an expression of pastoral charity: a gift of self offered to a specific community at a particular moment in time in which the good news of Christ is proclaimed, the content of the faith is presented, and the response of faith, conversion, unity, and holiness is inspired and actualized. Nuptial preaching manifests love, strengthens the bond, and encourages fruitfulness. Love motivates preaching and the preacher.

Pastoral charity, received in priestly ordination, is both a gift of the Holy Spirit and a task to engage. It is, at once, already present and not yet fulfilled. Pastoral charity continues to deepen in the life of the priest through his encounter with Christ and with Christ's holy people. As pastoral charity possesses a spousal character, the insights from chapter 1 regarding spousal love can be applied to the love which motivates preaching.

Summarizing the authors explored in the first chapter of this book, conjugal or spousal love is an activity of the whole person. It is not simply an act of the will, an expression of emotion, or a response to a biological imperative, though it involves all three. Conjugal love in marriage reflects a deliberate and exclusive choice. It is a complete gift of self, an intimate relationship, and a total offering and oblation. Spousal love unites the partners in a bond which provides the setting for growth and development, fruitfulness, and sanctification. For this love to endure, it must be protected, cherished, and nurtured by the partners through forgiveness, attentive communication, and passionate respect. These characteristics of spousal love further illuminate the facets of pastoral charity and the love which motivates the preacher.

The motivation for preaching is love. Preachers preach for the love of God and the love of God's people. The nuptial hermeneutic for preaching envisions every preaching act, regardless of the specific focus of the homily, as an expression of love. It seeks to unify, enable fruitfulness, and strengthen the community and the preacher. When the preacher is motivated by love and the assembly recognizes and receives this love, the preaching act is unitive and fruitful. As love motivates the relationship between the priest and the church, so also love motivates the expression of that love in the nuptial vision of preaching.

---

60. See John Paul II, *Pastores Dabo Vobis*, 21–23; 57–59.

Summary of the Preacher

The nuptial vision of preaching impacts the preacher's identity, authority, and motivation. The bridegroom preacher is motivated by love; demonstrates receptive, unitive, and generative dimensions in his identity; and exercises the authority of a fellow disciple, an official representative, and a relational partner. The love of the bridegroom preacher for the bridal assembly is expressed in the homily.

THE HOMILY

The third constitutive part of the preaching act is the homily. Much like mystery, the liturgical homily evades precise definition though it allows description.[61] In the nuptial hermeneutic, the homily expresses the spousal love of the preacher for the assembly. The act of preaching is a gift of self through which the preacher shares not only the gospel, but his very life (1 Thess 2:3). Characterized by kenotic vulnerability, in the homily the preacher interprets the scriptures, proclaims the mysteries of the faith, testifies to the power of the gospel, consoles and comforts the wounded, both confronts and offers challenge, invites the response of continued conversion, and leads to celebration. The nuptial hermeneutic understands the homily to be both the expression of love and one fruit of the relationship between the preacher and the assembly. This vision of the homily is assisted by attention to homiletical forms, attention to core concerns as found in the discipline of negotiation science and discussed later in this section, and attention to language through the use of metadiscourse, which refers to words and phrases that both involve and guide the hearers.

Homiletical Forms

The first dimension of the homily to be explored is the homiletical form. Form refers to the basic arrangement of material presented in a homily.[62] The form of a homily constitutes a critical aspect of preparation and presentation. A homiletical form is selected or developed with an eye to the gifts and personality of the preacher, the shape and content of the sacred text, and the unique and complex identity of a particular assembly. It is not expected that a preacher would always employ the same homiletical form for every preaching event. For the nuptial hermeneutic, the variety of homiletical forms offers

---

61. *Fulfilled in Your Hearing*, *Preaching the Mystery of Faith*, and the *Homiletic Directory* all offer different, yet complementary definitions of the liturgical homily.

62. McClure, *Preaching Words*, 38.

the bridegroom preacher an opportunity to present the homiletical gift to the bridal assembly in a way that inspires receptivity, expresses love, and enables fruitfulness. The three forms presented in this section are not the only ones suitable for the nuptial hermeneutic but are offered as fitting examples.

The first homiletical form to be examined is provided by James Henry Harris. He proposes a homiletical form rooted in the Hegelian dialectic of thesis-antithesis-synthesis which he calls "dialectic textuality."[63] In its most basic expression, a thesis about the world, God, the scriptural text, or some aspect of theology or doctrine is presented. An antithesis which contradicts or negates the thesis is offered. The antithesis provides questions, difficulties or possible inadequacies in regard to the thesis. The synthesis offers a mediation between the two positions and provides a lens through which these two seemingly contradictory viewpoints can be viewed and respected. To this dialectic, Harris contributes a "relevant question that grows out of the tension created between the thesis and antithesis [which] must be posed and answered in the synthesis."[64] In this form, either the thesis or the antithesis can be presented first; however, the synthesis would always come at the end and be preceded by the relevant question. The benefit of this homiletical form for the nuptial hermeneutic is that it respects and addresses alternate viewpoints through antithesis, proposes an idea in the thesis, invites the participation of the assembly with the relevant question, and accompanies the assembly into the synthesis. This homiletical form would be effective when confusing or controversial texts or doctrines are addressed; for example, the passage from Ephesians 5 regarding marriage is a controversial text.

A second homiletical form suitable to the nuptial hermeneutic is rooted in the philosophical hermeneutics of Paul Ricoeur and presented by Pablo A. Jiménez. He provides the homiletical form "Moving from the First Naiveté through Critical Reflection to Second Naiveté."[65] In this form, the homily begins with a pre-critical view of a topic, text, or doctrine. Initially, this form presents a surface reading of the text, broad but not deep. The textual picture is painted with broad strokes of the brush. The second movement in this form is critical reflection. At this point the doctrine, text, situation, or practice is investigated for difficulties, contradictions, implications, or worldviews. This is a deeper analysis which notices nuance, complexity, and depth. There is something destabilizing about critical reflection; it takes the simple picture and reveals the shades of color and meaning. The process of critical reflection requires trust on the part of the preacher and the assembly. In the final

---

63. Harris, "Thesis-Antithesis-Synthesis," 37.
64. Harris, "Thesis-Antithesis-Synthesis," 37.
65. Jiménez, "Moving from First Naiveté through Critical Reflection," 98.

movement, second naiveté, the preacher and the assembly return to the text after the journey through critical reflection. The landscape has not changed, but the perception and appreciation of it has. The first part of this structure brings the assembly and the preacher to the world of the text. Critical reflection brings the questions and concerns from the world of the assembly into the text. Following the process of critical reflection, the discoveries are brought into the world of the assembly. This homiletical form is fitting for the nuptial hermeneutic because the preacher and assembly are companions on the journey through this text. This form would be effective when approaching a familiar text; for example, the parable of the good Samaritan (Luke 10:25–37) or of the prodigal son (Luke 15:11–32).

Frank A. Thomas offers a third homiletical form, "From Problem through Gospel Assurance to Celebration."[66] In this form, the homily begins with a complicating problem in the world of the congregation. This problem can be from the scriptural text, a theological or doctrinal issue, or a circumstance in contemporary experience. The problem is admitted honestly and explored diligently, engaging the intellect, will, and emotions. Following this exploration, the homily moves to gospel assurance. In this section, "the preacher helps the church recognize how God's unconditional love and God's universal will for justice help the church interpret the complication and determine how to respond to it."[67] The problem is met by the good news. Gospel assurance, through doctrine, practice, and exegetical insight, inspires and empowers the assembly in their response. The promise of gospel assurance encourages a renewed vision and resolution. The final move in this form is celebration: an emotive proclamation of God's mighty action. This section is not exhortation; it is proclamation. God is the actor, healer, and deliverer. For the nuptial hermeneutic, this form of preaching assists to address wounds, scandals, and controversies. Because this homiletical form is rooted in divine action rather than human response, this form is particularly helpful when trust has been compromised, as is the situation with the most recent (2018 to present) abuse scandal.

The three homiletical forms presented by Harris, Jiménez, and Thomas offer the nuptial hermeneutic fitting examples of a structure for presentation and proclamation. Each form involves the assembly as a relational partner in which they are invited to join in synthesis, new appreciation, and celebration. Any homiletical form that engages the active receptivity of the assembly and invites their cooperation and response is useful for the nuptial

---

66. Thomas, "From Problem through Gospel Assurance to Celebration," 43–44.
67. Thomas, "From Problem through Gospel Assurance to Celebration," 43.

vision of preaching. Through homiletical forms such as these, the preacher approaches the assembly not as the teacher, but as the bridegroom.

The use of homiletical forms provides a structure for the preaching act. In the next section, the contribution of negotiation science to homiletical content will be explored.

Addressing Core Concerns

Moving from the form of the homily to its content, the next section applies the insights of negotiation science to the homily. The discipline of negotiation science offers the nuptial hermeneutic an understanding of the core emotional concerns of persons and, by extension, assemblies. Attention to these core concerns in the homily invites and enables the members of the assembly to receive and render the homiletical gift fruitful.

In their book *Beyond Reason: Using Emotions as You Negotiate*, Roger Fisher and Daniel Shapiro enumerate five core concerns that affect emotions. Noting that emotions are always present, powerful, and can be difficult to manage, these authors propose that positive emotions are encouraged by attention to core concerns. Positive emotions inspire cooperation, enhance the relationship, and protect the partners from exploitation.[68] In the nuptial hermeneutic, positive emotions encourage a healthy vulnerability, deepen the bond between the preacher and assembly, and enable fruitfulness.

Core concerns are "human wants that are important to almost everyone," and provide "a powerful framework to deal with emotions without getting overwhelmed by them."[69] Core concerns stimulate emotions. The five core concerns explored by Fisher and Shapiro are "*appreciation, affiliation, autonomy, status,* and *role.*"[70]

Appreciation, the first core concern, expresses value to the relational partner: their time, presence, and contribution are valued. Obstacles that inhibit appreciation center on the other's point of view. If the other's vantage is misunderstood or criticized without any expressed affirmation, then they experience unappreciation. Appreciation is expressed when the pont of view of the other is understood; when merit is found in the actions, thoughts, and feelings of the other; and when this understanding and merit is communicated through actions and words.[71] Appreciation is the founda-

---

68. Fisher and Shapiro, *Beyond Reason*, 6–8.
69. Fisher and Shapiro, *Beyond Reason*, 16.
70. Fisher and Shapiro, *Beyond Reason*, 16.
71. Fisher and Shapiro, *Beyond Reason*, 27–28.

tional core concern. In the nuptial hermeneutic, appreciation manifests the fundamental equality between the preacher and assembly.

The second core concern is affiliation; it is the sense of honest connection and emotional closeness between relational partners. Affiliation is built through structural and personal connections. Structural connections are those which bind a person to a group or community. Personal connections attract and tie to a particular individual. Structural connections revolve around background, belief, common activities, age, education, family, and cultural similarities. Personal connections are built through contact, sharing of ideas and goals, and the sharing of life together.[72] For the nuptial hermeneutic, the relationship is both structural and personal. Affiliation promotes and enhances the relational reciprocity between the assembly and the preacher.

Autonomy, the third core concern, regards a person's freedom to receive, decide, and act. Fisher and Shapiro promote the importance of expanding one's autonomy while not imposing on the other's. Autonomy is expanded by making recommendations and suggestions. The autonomy of the other is respected through consultation and clarification.[73] In the nuptial hermeneutic, the principles of fundamental equality, relational reciprocity, stable relationship, and serving the *koinonia* are enhanced through an appropriate respect for autonomy. This core concern is respected when the homily is presented in the language of invitation rather than command.

Status, the fourth core concern, "refers to our standing in comparison to our standing with others."[74] Attention to this core concern begins with the recognition of human dignity and extends to respect for opinion, expertise, social, political, and religious office. Recognizing status is not about subservience or submission; it is about respect and recognition.[75] Recognizing status reinforces the principles of fundamental equality and relational reciprocity while enhancing the stable relationship, serving the *koinonia*, and promoting fruitfulness.

Experiencing a fulfilling role is the fifth and final core concern. Fisher and Shapiro note three qualities of a fulfilling role: clarity of purpose, personally meaningful, and not a pretense.[76] A fulfilling role is a share in the mission; it indicates that one is a participant rather than a spectator. For the nuptial hermeneutic, a fulfilling role is a fruit of the homily. When the relational partners in the preaching act express appreciation, experience affiliation, respect

---

72. Fisher and Shapiro, *Beyond Reason*, 53–55.
73. Fisher and Shapiro, *Beyond Reason*, 93.
74. Fisher and Shapiro, *Beyond Reason*, 95.
75. Fisher and Shapiro, *Beyond Reason*, 95–110.
76. Fisher and Shapiro, *Beyond Reason*, 117–18.

each other's autonomy, and acknowledge the dignity and status of the other, then sharing in a common mission through a diversity of roles is possible.

The five core concerns offered by Fisher and Shapiro from the discipline of negotiation science provide the nuptial hermeneutic a method for understanding the deep emotional desires of the assembly. Attention to these core concerns in the homily enables the preacher and the assembly to deepen their relationship and become fruitful. The next section addresses the language through which these core concerns and the other aspects of the nuptial hermeneutic are presented.

Metadiscourse

The homily is a language event: the words are critical. They can provide information, convey and inspire emotion, soften and harden hearts, incite violence, and cultivate justice and peace. Words are powerful. The language of the homily in the nuptial hermeneutic expresses love, unity, reciprocity, deepens the bond, enables fruitfulness, and serves the communion. The concept of metadiscourse from the field of linguistics offers the spousal vision of preaching a method to engage and involve the assembly through the words and phrases in the homily.[77] The following paragraphs provide an introduction to the concept of metadiscourse and an examination of the interactive and interactional dimensions.

In his work *Metadiscourse: Exploring Interaction in Writing*, Ken Hyland provides a careful analysis of the concept, history, and utilization of metadiscourse.[78] Hyland offers the following definition: "Metadiscourse is the cover term for the self-reflective expressions used to negotiate interactional meanings in a text, assisting the writer (or speaker) to express a viewpoint and engage with readers as members of a particular community."[79] Metadiscourse is language that reveals the author or speaker and involves the reader or hearer. It is distinct from the information or propositions made, expresses the interactions between the writer and the reader, and distinguishes between events occurring within the presentation and those occurring outside of it. Metadiscoursal words or phrases frame and support the information conveyed. They demonstrate the concern of the author to involve the reader. They clarify the world within the discourse itself and the world of the assembly.[80]

Hyland utilizes two overarching dimensions of metadiscourse: the interactive and the interactional. The interactive dimension responds to the

---

77. See Malmström, "Engaging the Congregation," 561–82.
78. Hyland, *Metadiscourse: Exploring Interaction in Writing*, 43–64.
79. Hyland, *Metadiscourse: Exploring Interaction in Writing*, 43–44.
80. Hyland, *Metadiscourse: Exploring Interaction in Writing*, 43–53.

needs, interests, and knowledge of the receiver. These phrases guide the reader through the discourse. Hyland notes that the use of metadiscoursal resources in the interactive dimension "addresses ways of organizing discourse, rather than experience, and reveals the extent to which the text is constructed with the readers' needs in mind."[81] The interactional dimension expresses the author's views and position in regard to elements of the discourse. The interactional dimension reveals the author, promotes solidarity, and involves the reader in the text. Metadiscoursal phrases offer guidance and promote engagement.[82]

Table 3.3 Metadiscourse[83]

Category	Function	Examples
Interactive	*Help to guide the reader through the text*	*Resources*
Transitions	Express relations between main clauses	In addition; but; thus; and
Frame Markers	Refer to discourse acts, sequences, or stages	Finally; to conclude; my purpose is
Endophoric Markers	Refer to information in other parts of the text	Noted above; see Fig; in section 2
Evidentials	Refer to information from other texts	According to X; Z states
Code Glosses	Elaborate propositional meanings	Namely; e.g.; such as; in other words
Interactional	*Involve the reader in the text*	*Resources*
Hedges	Withhold commitment and open dialogue	Might; perhaps; possible; about
Boosters	Emphasize certainty or close dialogue	In fact; definitely; it is clear that
Attitude markers	Express writer's attitude to proposition	Unfortunately; I agree, surprisingly
Self-mentions	Explicit reference to the author(s)	I; we; my; me; our
Engagement Markers	Explicitly build relationship with the reader	Consider; note; you can see that

81. Hyland, *Metadiscourse: Exploring Interaction in Writing*, 57.
82. Hyland, *Metadiscourse: Exploring Interaction in Writing*, 57–58.
83. *Source*: Hyland, *Metadiscourse: Exploring Interaction in Writing*, Table 3.1 on page 58.

There are five principle linguistic resources or markers proposed by Hyland for each of the two dimensions: interactive and interactional. The interactive markers, which provide guidance to the receiver, include transitions, frame markers, endophoric markers, evidentials, and code glosses. Transitions connect information and points within the discourse. Examples of transitions are: *therefore, similarly, moreover, on the contrary,* and *consequently*. Frame markers indicate goals and signal shifts or sequences. These include *my purpose is, I argue that, for these reasons, to conclude,* and *finally*. Endophoric markers are words or phrases that make reference to other parts of the same discourse or work. In speech these would include phrases such as *as we said, noted previously, earlier we noted*. The markers help to summarize and promote coherence. Evidentials are references from other texts: *Saint Paul says, the Gospel recounts, our faith teaches*. Evidentials are appeals to authority. The fifth linguistic resource provided by Hyland is code glosses. These are usually parenthetical statements offering clarification, rephrasing, or elaboration. Some examples of code glosses are *in other words, for example, this is defined as, namely*. The five interactive resources guide the reader or listener through the text of the discourse. They manifest the concern of the author to engage the reader or hearer as a relational partner.[84]

In addition to the markers for the interactive dimension, Hyland provides five linguistic markers or resources for the interactional dimension. Providing involvement for the reader or listener as well as the author's perspective, these markers include hedges, boosters, attitude markers, self-mentions, and engagement markers. Hedges, such as *possibly, perhaps,* and *might*, allow the possibility of alternate viewpoints and visions. The use of hedges respects the recipient's autonomy to evaluate an idea or concept. Boosters, words such as *obviously, clearly,* and *certainly*, are designed to restrict alternatives or conflicting views. These are utilized when the author desires to express confidence or certainty. Attitude markers convey the affective stance of the author in regard to a proposition; these are usually verbs such as *prefer* or *agree*, adverbs such as *unfortunately* and *hopefully*, and adjectives including *logical, remarkable,* and *appropriate*. Self-mentions are direct references to the author using *I, we, me, our,* or *my*. The careful use of self-mentions reveals the personality and stance of the author. Engagement markers are the fifth resource for the interactional dimension. These words and phrases, *consider, you can see that, please note, you, your,* and the inclusive *we*, directly address the reader or listener; they build the relationship between the speaker and the listener. While the interactive markers guide the listener through the discourse, the interactional markers involve

---

84. Hyland, *Metadiscourse: Exploring Interaction in Writing*, 59–61.

the listener in the text of the discourse. They demonstrate the desire of the author to invite the recipients to participate in the language event.[85]

Metadiscourse offers the nuptial hermeneutic and the bridegroom preacher an approach to the language employed in the homily. Attending to the interactive and interactional markers allows the preacher to guide the assembly through the homily and invite their active participation in the preaching event.

Summary of the Homily

The bridegroom preacher expresses his spousal love for the bridal assembly through the homily. The selection of homiletical forms, attention to emotional core concerns, and the use of metadiscoursal words and phrases assist the nuptial hermeneutic to present the homiletical gift. The form, attention, and language of the homily engage the assembly as a relational partner, strengthen the bond between the preacher and the assembly, and enables fruitfulness. The homily is a nuptial encounter. In the final section of this chapter, the method of preparation for this sacred encounter, the homiletical method, will be examined.

HOMILETICAL METHOD

The homiletical method engages the seven characteristics or principles of the nuptial hermeneutic as a program for homily preparation. As explored earlier in this chapter, these principles impact the understandings of the assembly, the preacher, and the homily. This section reviews these seven principles, gathers the insights provided in the earlier sections, and outlines a strategy for preparing a homily. The method of the nuptial hermeneutic brings together insights and themes which would be found in marriage preparation, a priest retreat, a marriage enrichment conference, and a wedding reception.

The Seven Principles

The first principle of the nuptial hermeneutic is the fundamental equality between the preacher and the members of the assembly. All are disciples of the Lord; together, the preacher and the assembly constitute a *we*. The first principle concerns unity.

---

85. Hyland, *Metadiscourse: Exploring Interaction in Writing*, 61–64.

The second principle is asymmetrical or relational reciprocity. The priest and the members of the assembly live in relationship to each other through their dual participation in the one priesthood of Christ. The ministerial priesthood of the ordained and the royal priesthood of the baptized are ordered to each other and depend on each other to flourish. The preacher and the assembly join together as a *you and me*. The second principle is grounded in relationship.

The third principle of the nuptial hermeneutic is that the motivation is love. Preaching is motivated by love and preaching is received in love. The loving relationship between the preacher and the assembly animates their homiletical life together. The third principle clarifies motivation.

The fourth principle states that spousal preaching occurs in the context of a stable relationship. Like Saint Peter Chrysologus, Saint Augustine, Saint John Chrysostom, and Saint Francis de Sales, the priest is the regular preacher for this assembly. He is not a visitor or a traveling missionary. The relationship between the preacher and the assembly requires time to develop and mature. The fourth principle affirms stability.

The fifth principle of the nuptial hermeneutic is a supportive spirituality. Found at the intersection of spiritualities of marriage and spiritualities of the ministerial priesthood, the nuptial homiletical spirituality builds communion, both temporal and supernatural, through the affirmation of identity, loving attention, patient expectation, and local dedication. The fifth principle concerns support.

The sixth principle is fruitfulness. The union between the preacher and the assembly has generative power. The fourfold fruitfulness is doxological, spiritual, vocational, and homiletical. This principle recognizes that preaching both expresses a loving relationship and is a fruit of the relationship. The sixth principle encourages fruitfulness.

The seventh principle of the nuptial hermeneutic is service to the *koinonia*. Preaching serves, supports, and strengthens a deep interpersonal relationship between the preacher and the assembly. Analogous to the good of the spouses in marriage, the *koinonia* provides a home for mutual growth and flourishing. The seventh principle supports communion.

The seven principles include the following: unity, relationship, motivation, stability, support, fruitfulness, and communion. These principles guide the bridegroom preacher's exploration of the assembly, the scriptural texts, and the preparation of the homily for each preaching event. Before presenting a strategy for preparation, it is helpful to summarize the insights gained from the analysis of the assembly, the preacher, and the homily.

Fruitful Insights

The encounter between the seven principles of the nuptial hermeneutic presented above and the homiletical components of the assembly, the preacher, and the homily produces various fruits. These fruits include a new vision for the identity of each component, the assistance of perspectives from within the field of homiletics and other disciplines, and the modification of aspects of these components by the nuptial hermeneutic.

According to the nuptial vision of preaching, the assembly is the bride. The bridal assembly is recognized as an equal partner in the preaching relationship. The discipline of congregational exegesis assists the nuptial hermeneutic through the symbolic and theological analyses of the assembly. Utilizing these insights, the bridegroom preacher comes to know the complexity of the bride. The discipline of reader- or listener-response criticism honors the bride's receptivity. This perspective acknowledges that the interpretation of the homily occurs within the assembly. The counsels of reader or listener-response criticism enable the preacher to anticipate and assist the interpretive activity of the congregation. The womanist perspective offers the preacher a method to care for the wounds in the assembly. The preacher engages in this delicate work through affirmation, sensitivity, the honoring of tradition and history, and the proclamation of liberation and healing in Christ. Congregational exegesis, reader or listener-response criticism, and the womanist perspective assist the bridegroom preacher to know, honor, and care for the bridal assembly.

The preacher is the bridegroom. The principles of the nuptial hermeneutic impact the understanding of the preacher's identity, authority, and motivation. There are three dimensions to the preacher's identity: receptive, unitive, and generative. The bridegroom listens to the word of the Lord and the voice of the bride receiving both his identity and mission. Expressing the unitive dimension, the preacher offers a complete gift of self to the bride through the homily. The unitive dimension flows into the generative dimension where the bond between the bridegroom and the bride is strengthened and the relationship is made fruitful. The exercise of authority by the preacher within this relationship is filial, official, and relational. He is a disciple in virtue of baptism, an apostle by ordination and appointment, and a relational partner by the consent of the bridal assembly. The third level of authority is a gift by the assembly given in response to the gift by the preacher. Love motivates the preacher's gift. Every other homiletical goal extends from the primacy of love. The nuptial hermeneutic animates the motivation, clarifies the authority, and crystalizes the identity of the bridegroom preacher.

The homily is an expression of the spousal love of the bridegroom preacher for the bridal assembly. The nuptial hermeneutic is assisted by the selection of homiletical forms, attention to emotional core concerns, and the use of metadiscoursal language. The form of the homily encourages active receptivity by the members of the assembly. A form that regards the assembly as a relational partner and invites their cooperation and participation is suitable for the nuptial hermeneutic. The discipline of negotiation science offers the concept of emotional core concerns. Attention to appreciation, affiliation, autonomy, status, and role in the homily encourages the members of the assembly to receive the message of the preacher. Metadiscoursal language guides the listener through the homily and invites his or her involvement in the preaching event. The form of the homily, attention to emotional core concerns, and the use of metadiscoural words and phrases in the homily honors the dignity of the bridal assembly as a relational partner, encourages receptivity, and enables fruitfulness.

The impact of the encounter between the nuptial hermeneutic and the assembly, the preacher and the homily offers multiple insights and tools for the bridegroom preacher. Attention to these fruits inspires the preparation of the homily in the nuptial vision.

Strategy for Preparation

This final section provides a strategy for preparing a homily utilizing the nuptial vision.[86] There are six steps in the homiletical method rooted in the nuptial hermeneutic. This strategy for preparation begins with the expression of the preacher's intention and follows with contemplation, formulation, presentation, reception, and transformation. These six steps are outlined in this section.

First, the preacher expresses his intention. The following formula provides an example. *My purpose is to proclaim the good news of Jesus Christ out of love for God and love for God's Holy People. I intend to approach the bridal assembly as my equal in the life of grace mindful of the gift and responsibility for the proclamation of the saving word of Christ and the teachings of the church. I seek to prepare and proclaim this homily for the glory of God and the benefit of this community. May my words be received and bear fruit as we approach the Wedding Feast of the Lamb.* Through this expression of intention, the preacher acknowledges the equality of the assembly, the reciprocity of the relationship, the motivation, and the power of the homily for unity and fruitfulness.

86. Two sample homilies are included in the appendix.

The second step of this strategy is contemplation. The bridegroom preacher contemplates the assembly and the sacred texts appointed for the particular liturgy. The insights of congregational exegesis, reader or listener-response criticism, and the womanist perspective guides the contemplation of the assembly. The bridegroom preacher seeks the demographic and theological diversity of the assembly, notes obstacles to receptivity, and names the wounds in the community. These facets of the assembly are then taken into the contemplation of the sacred text. The *Homiletical Directory* based on the *Catechism* notes three essential criteria for scriptural interpretation: the unity of the scripture, reading within the living tradition of the Church, and the analogy of faith or interrelation of the truths of the faith.[87] In addition to these three guidelines, the responsible bridegroom preacher utilizes every historical, exegetical, and interpretive method and approach at his disposal to gather the seeds of good news for the community. The contemplation by the preacher brings the community and the sacred texts together, preparing for their encounter in the liturgy and the homily.

The third step is formulation. Analogous to the gestation of a child, this takes time. Contemplation continues during this process as the seeds of good news are gathered and the needs of the assembly are revealed. When the bridegroom preacher arrives at a particular seed to plant, he chooses a homiletical form that involves the assembly and supports the homiletical focus. The preacher prepares the text of the homily, in writing or internally, attending to emotional core concerns and language. Attention to form, core concerns, and language facilitates the reception of the homily.

The fourth step is presentation, the actual preaching of the homily. The preacher renews his intention, makes a gift of self in the act of preaching, and offers the fruit of his contemplation and formulation to the assembly. In the act of preaching, the bridegroom preacher models kenotic vulnerability for the assembly. He shares not only his message but his very life.

The fifth step in the homiletical method is reception by the assembly and the preacher. The reception by the assembly (and the preacher) expresses the kenotic vulnerability of the preacher because he surrenders the interpretation of his words to the members of the assembly. He is, at the same time, a receiver of this homily because this is likely the only homily that he will hear on this day. The focus of the homiletical method in the nuptial hermeneutic is reception, not proclamation.

The final step is transformation. This is the fruit of preaching and not of a particular homily. The bridegroom preacher and the bridal assembly build

---

87. Congregation for Divine Worship and the Discipline of the Sacraments, *Homiletic Directory*, 17.

a homiletical life together. They listen together to the word proclaimed and they speak to each other within the liturgy and outside of the liturgy. As the bridegroom preacher models kenotic vulnerability in his life and preaching, the assembly is inspired to respond in kenotic vulnerability. In a relationship of *mutual kenotic vulnerability*, inspired and supported through preaching in the nuptial hermeneutic, the preacher and the assembly journey together toward the life of the blessed.

Summary of Homiletical Method

The journey together toward the life of the blessed is the ultimate goal of a homiletical method. The six steps examined here outline the strategy for preparation for preaching utilizing the nuptial hermeneutic. The first three steps, intention, contemplation, and formulation, are primarily actions of the preacher. The fourth step, presentation, and the fifth step, reception, are relational and unitive activities of the preacher and the assembly. The sixth step, transformation, manifests both the bond and the fruit of this spousal relationship. These six steps foster a method of preparation for preaching that strengthens the bond between the preacher and the community and enables fruitfulness.

CONCLUSION

The spousal relationship between the priest and the church is expressed and strengthened through preaching. This chapter explored nuptiality as a theological category, proposed seven characteristics of the nuptial hermeneutic for preaching, and examined the four components of the preaching act in light of this hermeneutic. This chapter, and this book, concludes with a strategy for preaching using this nuptial vision.

In this book we have examined the relationship between husband and wife, the analogous spousal relationship between the priest and the church, and explored how the nuptial vision can impact and enhance the preaching ministry. In the appendix which follows, I have provided a one-page summary of the strategy for preaching, a rubric for evaluating homilies rooted in the affective experience of the assembly, and two sample homilies.

Preaching is a relational act. We preach in the context of a relationship. Whenever we deepen our understanding of this relationship, we renew our preaching and we are renewed as preachers who echo the Voice of the Bridegroom.

Strategy for Preparation in the Nuptial Hermeneutic

I. Express your intention.

   A. Sample formula: *My purpose is to proclaim the good news of Jesus Christ out of love for God and love for God's Holy People. I intend to approach the bridal assembly as my equal in the life of grace mindful of the gift and responsibility for the proclamation of the saving word of Christ and the teachings of the church. I seek to prepare and proclaim this homily for the glory of God and the benefit of this community. May my words be received and bear fruit as we approach the Wedding Feast of the Lamb.*

II. Contemplation

   A. Of the Assembly

      1. What stories have I heard in the parish in the past two weeks? What are the major themes?

      2. What are the major events in the parish last week or planned for this week? Is there a national or world or church event?

      3. What are the main struggles, difficulties, or wounds I have heard about or observed in the past two weeks?

      4. Who is feeling left out or neglected in the parish?

   B. Of the Scriptures

      1. Bring the contemplative fruits from the assembly to your contemplation of the scriptures.

2. What do the texts say? What do the texts say to me? What do the texts say to the situation of this parish?

C. Harvest the fruits of this double contemplation and select one (or some) for the homily.

III. Formulation

A. How is the homily organized? Does it invite the listeners to engage the message?

B. Does the homily recognize the dignity and freedom of the assembly and offer them ways or a way to accept and later respond to the message?

C. Do my words offer the listeners guidance through the structure of the homily and invite their internal participation?

IV. Presentation

A. Before the liturgy, renew your intention for preaching. The sample formula above is appropriate.

B. Offer the gift of your homily to the assembly with attention, reverence and love.

Homily Evaluation Rubric Survey

1. I was able to follow this homily.
   Strongly Disagree 1 2 3 4 5 6 7 8 9 10 Strongly Agree
2. This preacher speaks to my life.
   Strongly Disagree 1 2 3 4 5 6 7 8 9 10 Strongly Agree
3. I learned something in the homily.
   Strongly Disagree 1 2 3 4 5 6 7 8 9 10 Strongly Agree
4. This preacher challenges me.
   Strongly Disagree 1 2 3 4 5 6 7 8 9 10 Strongly Agree
5. This preacher cares about his congregation.
   Strongly Disagree 1 2 3 4 5 6 7 8 9 10 Strongly Agree
6. I felt like this homily was just for me.
   Strongly Disagree 1 2 3 4 5 6 7 8 9 10 Strongly Agree
7. This preacher understands my life.
   Strongly Disagree 1 2 3 4 5 6 7 8 9 10 Strongly Agree
8. This homily helps me to live my faith.
   Strongly Disagree 1 2 3 4 5 6 7 8 9 10 Strongly Agree
9. I was comforted by this homily.
   Strongly Disagree 1 2 3 4 5 6 7 8 9 10 Strongly Agree
10. This homily gives me hope.
    Strongly Disagree 1 2 3 4 5 6 7 8 9 10 Strongly Agree

Two Sample Homilies

The two homilies provided in this appendix were preached at Our Lady of Lourdes Catholic Church in Monroe, NC where I serve as pastor. Both homilies were prepared utilizing the nuptial hermeneutic for preaching. The dates and pericopes are included with each homily.

Homily for the 20th Sunday in Ordinary Time, Year B

Prov 9:1–9; Pss 34:2–3, 4–5, 6–7, 9a; Eph 5:15–20; John 6:51–58

August 19, 2018

I may have mentioned, once or twice, my goddaughter. She is a little more than three and a half. A few weeks ago, when the calendars of a busy three-and-a-half-year-old and a busy parish priest aligned, I met Madeline and her family at one of the newly constructed eateries near Charlotte. The family arrived first and were seated and beginning to eat when I walked through the door of the restaurant. My goddaughter immediately got up from her chair, ran toward me cheerfully saying the closest and cutest approximation of Father Benjamin that she can must muster, and jumped into my open arms. The joy in her eyes and the smile on her face were sharp contrasts to the angry and concerned eyes and disapproving looks of the other people seated in the restaurant. I saw their faces and I knew why they looked the way that they did: they were horrified and concerned to see a priest holding a child. I imagine that it will be that way for the rest of my life.

If there was any trust left after the scandals revealed in 2002, and if any trust had been rebuilt in the sixteen years since then, it is now gone. I am utterly horrified. I am ashamed. I am brokenhearted. I am angry. I am disappointed. I am furious that consecrated men abused children and young people, that they abused their authority and the trust of their sacred office. I am horrified that predators were promoted rather than being punished. It's tough to preach, and it is tough to pray.

But let us be clear: I and other faithful priests are not the victims here. We are, at best, collateral damage. The victims are the young people and children who were violated by those who should have protected them. The victims are those who were rejected and neglected by church and legal systems. They are the ones who need prayers and support. They are the ones who deserve our compassion, consolation, and care. Our eyes can never look away from those who are suffering, because to do so would be to take our eyes off of the Suffering Savior.

This is not a time of persecution: it is a season of purification. We as a church must face the examination of conscience and the examination of conduct. This will not be pretty. The depths of depravity and dishonesty must be brought to the light. It will be painful. It will be disappointing and disheartening. But we pray that it will also be purifying and healing.

Knowledge and admission of sin and a desire to reform are the first steps on the path to holiness, and holiness is our only option. There is no path forward that does not involve a deeper commitment and relationship with Jesus Christ. We need an investigation and a review board and screenings and policies. Those must be part of the process, and they will be. But there is no abiding change, no change of heart or change of practice or change of behavior without a change of direction from the ways of the world to the way of the Lord Jesus. Holiness is our only answer. Holiness is our only path. Holiness is the only credible witness that can testify before the victims of abuse and the world. We have no choice. We must seek to be holy.

There is a great consolation in our long history. In the times of greatest disobedience and debauchery, in the days when faithfulness is cast aside, and sin is set up as the ideal, it is in those times when God raises up his greatest saints. I am consoled that in the face of these scandals the purifying fire of God's justice will make way for the glorifying power of God's holiness. God will raise up his saints. God will raise up his witnesses. The ever-faithful God remains ever-faithful and ever-merciful. That is our consolation and our challenge.

You see, it is from this room and from this community, that God will raise up his saints. We will support each other on the way of holiness. As a priest, I cannot become holy without you. I am not a hermit, nor a monk. My path to holiness is not a cave in the desert nor a cell in a monastery; it is here, with you and for you. We walk the road to the kingdom together.

We struggle to be holy together. And together, with the trust and joy and expectation of a child of God, we run to the open arms of Jesus.

Homily for the 3rd Sunday in Ordinary Time, Year C

Neh 8:2–4a, 5–6, 8–10; Ps 19:8, 9, 10, 15; 1 Cor 12:12–30;

Luke 1:1–4; 4:14–21

January 27, 2019

Ten years ago, today, one of my seminary classmates died quite unexpectedly. Deacon Adam Crowe, of the Diocese of Ogdensburg and only twenty-six years old, died a few months before he was to be ordained a priest. He was only sick for few days. We heard much later that it was some kind of heart infection that caused his death. Deacon Adam was the nicest one in my class. It was very difficult for us after he passed away. Today my classmates are sending messages and posting memories of Deacon Adam on social media. Every member of my class who was ordained to the priesthood is still in ministry. All of us are still preaching today.

A little more than fourteen hundred years ago, a monk in Rome was given a new mission by the pope. Leave Rome and go to England. Preach the gospel and establish the church. So the monk, whose name was Augustine (not Augustine the son of Saint Monica, but another Augustine), arrived in England and began to preach. His first words were very simple: We bring you good news.

"The Spirit of the Lord is upon me for he sent me to bring glad tidings to the poor." These are the words of Isaiah and the words of Jesus. The Lord has sent me to bring to the good news. That is the heart of the message. It is good news that Isaiah and Ezra and Nehemiah and Jesus proclaim. It is good news that we want to hear. It is good news that we need to hear.

I will never forget the morning after Deacon Adam died. One of the priests at the seminary sat in a room with my class and said, "Do not seek the living among the dead. Our brother is alive in Christ Jesus." It was good news that we needed to hear. It was good news that we wanted to hear. In the midst of sorrow, shock, disbelief, and disappointment, we needed to hear the good news. We bring you good news.

Our faith is good news. The gospel is good news. Even the law of God is good news. The great assembly in the days of Ezra and Nehemiah when the people heard the law for the first time in three generations caused both weeping and rejoicing. The people wept because they recognized their lack of faithfulness to God's law. They rejoiced because they recognized that

God loved them enough to speak to them. They might have heard some challenging words, but more than the challenge, they heard good news. We bring you good news.

We want the good news. We need the good news. There is too much sorrow and too much pain and too much violence and too much bad news. We want the good news. We need the good news. We bring you good news.

We bring you good news, for unto you this day in the city of David a Savior has been born for you who is Christ and Lord. We bring you good news.

We bring you good news, for the Spirit of the Lord is upon me and he has anointed me to bring the good news, to proclaim liberty to the captives, sight to the blind, freedom to the oppressed, and a year of jubilee. We bring you good news.

We bring you good news, for the wine is abundant at the wedding feast and the lost sheep, the lost coin, and the lost son are all found. We bring you good news.

We bring you good news, because no one need fear death for the savior's death has set us free. We shall not seek the living among the dead, for the good news of Jesus Christ claims victory over sin and death forever. We bring you good news.

We bring you good news. It is good news we proclaim. It is good news that we want. It is good news that we need. It is good news that we share.

And now Jesus feeds us. He tells us the good news and gathers us to his table. As he once did for his disciples, he now does for you and for me. He opens the scriptures. He breaks the bread and he sends us out to bring the good news. Amen.

Bibliography

Adams, Gwendolen. "The Importance of Geographic Stability for the Church." *Church Life Journal*, April 30, 2018. https://churchlifejournal.nd.edu/articles/the-importance-of-geographic-stability-for-the-church/.
Allen, Ronald James, ed. *Patterns of Preaching: A Sermon Sampler*. St. Louis: Chalice, 2006.
Anderson, Carl A., and José Granados. *Called to Love: Approaching John Paul II's Theology of the Body*. New York: Image, 2009.
Baker, Andrew R. "Here Comes the Groom—The Priest as the Bridegroom of the Church." *Lay Witness*, May 1, 2003. https://web.archive.org/web/20160726192121/http://www.cuf.org/2003/05/here-comes-the-groom-the-priest-as-the-bridegroom-of-the-church/.
Barth, Karl. *Homiletics*. Translated by Geoffrey W. Bromiley and Donald E. Daniels. Louisville: Westminster John Knox, 1991.
Benedict XV, Pope. *Humani Generis Redemptionem*. http://www.vatican.va/content/benedict-xv/en/encyclicals/documents/hf_ben-xv_enc_15061917_humani-generis-redemptionem.html.
Benedict XVI, Pope. *Sacramentum Caritatis*. http://www.vatican.va/content/benedict-xvi/en/apost_exhortations/documents/hf_ben-xvi_exh_20070222_sacramentum-caritatis.html.
———. *Verbum Domini*. http://www.vatican.va/content/benedict-xvi/en/apost_exhortations/documents/hf_ben-xvi_exh_20100930_verbum-domini.html.
Berger, Alisha. "Study Finds a 7-Year Itch, and a 4-Year One." *New York Times*, October 5, 1999. http://www.nytimes.com/1999/10/05/health/study-finds-a-7-year-itch-and-a-4-year-one.html.
Bransfield, J. Brian. *The Human Person: According to John Paul II*. Boston: Pauline, 2010.
Buber, Martin. *I and Thou: Martin Buber; A New Translation with a Prologue "I and You" and Notes*. Translated by Walter A. Kaufmann. New York: Simon & Schuster, 1996.
Burke, Cormac. *Man and Values: A Personalist Anthropology*. New York: Scepter, 2007.

———. *The Theology of Marriage: Personalism, Doctrine, and Canon Law*. Washington, DC: Catholic University of America, 2015.
Butler, Sara. *The Catholic Priesthood and Women: A Guide to the Teaching of the Church*. Chicago: Hillenbrand, 2007.
———. "The Priest as Sacrament of Christ the Bridegroom." *Worship* 66.6 (November 1992) 498–517.
Byrne, Brendan. *Life Abounding: A Reading of John's Gospel*. Collegeville: Liturgical, 2014.
Cahall, Perry J. *The Mystery of Marriage: A Theology of the Body and the Sacrament*. Chicago: Hillenbrand, 2016.
Center for the Applied Research in the Apostolate. "Frequently Requested Church Statistics." https://cara.georgetown.edu/frequently-requested-church-statistics/.
Code of Canon Law. Washington, DC: USCCB, 1983.
Collins, Raymond. *Second Corinthians*. Paideia: Commentaries on the New Testament. Grand Rapids: Baker Academic, 2013.
Congregation for Divine Worship and the Discipline of the Sacraments. *Homiletic Directory*. Washington, DC: USCCB, 2015.
Congregation for the Clergy. *Directory on the Ministry and Life of Priests*. Washington, DC: USCCB, 1994.
Cozzens, Andrew H. "*Imago Vivens Iesu Christi Sponsi Ecclesiae*: The Priest as the Living Image of Jesus Christ the Bridegroom of the Church through the Evangelical Counsels." STD diss., Pontifical University of St. Thomas Aquinas, Rome, 2008.
Culp, Kristine A. *Vulnerability and Glory: A Theological Account*. Louisville: Westminster John Knox, 2010.
Dulles, Avery. *The Priestly Office: A Theological Reflection*. New York: Paulist, 1997.
Fisher, Helen. "Is There a Biological Basis for the 7-Year Itch?" *Scientific American*, January 1, 2015. https://www.scientificamerican.com/article/is-there-a-biological-basis-for-the-7-year-itch/.
Fisher, Roger, and Daniel Shapiro. *Beyond Reason: Using Emotions as You Negotiate*. New York: Penguin, 2006.
Flake, Elaine M. *God in Her Midst: Preaching Healing to Wounded Women*. Valley Forge: Judson, 2007.
Foley, Edward, ed. *A Handbook for Catholic Preaching*. Collegeville: Liturgical, 2016.
Fornés, Juan. "Commentary on Canon 1134." In *Exegetical Commentary on the Code of Canon Law*, 3/2:1523–26. Collection Gratianus Series. Annotated Legislative Texts. English Language ed. Montreal, Canada: Wilson & Lafleur, 2004.
Francis, Pope. *Amoris Latitia*. http://www.vatican.va/content/francesco/en/apost_exhortations/documents/papa-francesco_esortazione-ap_20160319_amoris-laetitia.html.
———. *Evangelii Gaudium*. http://www.vatican.va/content/francesco/en/apost_exhortations/documents/papa-francesco_esortazione-ap_20131124_evangelii-gaudium.html.
———. *Gaudete et Exultate*. http://www.vatican.va/content/francesco/en/apost_exhortations/documents/papa-francesco_esortazione-ap_20180319_gaudete-et-exsultate.html.
Galot, Jean. *Theology of the Priesthood*. Translated by Roger Balducelli. San Francisco: Ignatius, 2005.
Gandolfo, Elizabeth O'Donnell. *The Power and Vulnerability of Love: A Theological Anthropology*. Minneapolis: Fortress, 2015.

Gerring, John. *Social Science Methodology: A Unified Framework.* Cambridge: Cambridge University Press, 2013.
Harris, James Henry. "Thesis-Antithesis-Synthesis." In *Patterns of Preaching*, edited by Ronald Allen, 36–42. St. Louis: Chalice, 2006.
Hildebrand, Dietrich von. *Marriage: The Mystery of Faithful Love.* London: Longmans, Green, 1956.
Hoge, Dean R. *Experiences of Priests Ordained Five to Nine Years: A Report Published by the Seminary Department of the National Catholic Educational Association.* Edited by Bernard F. Stratman. Washington, DC: National Catholic Educational Association, 2006.
———. *The First Five Years of Priesthood: A Study of Newly Ordained Catholic Priests.* Collegeville: Liturgical, 2002.
Hyland, Ken. *Metadiscourse: Exploring Interactions in Writing.* Bloomsbury Classics in Linguistics. New York: Bloomsbury Academic, 2018.
Jiménez, Pablo A. "Moving from First Naiveté through Critical Reflection to Second Naiveté." In *Patterns of Preaching*, edited by Ronald Allen, 98–103. St. Louis: Chalice, 2006.
John Paul II, Pope. *Ecclesia de Eucharistia.* http://www.vatican.va/holy_father/special_features/encyclicals/documents/hf_jp-ii_enc_20030417_ecclesia_eucharistia_en.html.
———. *Gift and Mystery.* New York: Image, 1996.
———. *Letter to My Brother Priests, 1979–2001.* Princeton: Scepter, 2001.
———. *Man and Woman He Created Them: A Theology of the Body.* Edited by Michael Waldstein. Boston: Pauline, 2006.
———. *Mulieris Dignitatem.* http://www.vatican.va/content/john-paul-ii/en/apost_letters/1988/documents/hf_jp-ii_apl_19880815_mulieris-dignitatem.html.
———. *Pastores Dabo Vobis.* http://www.vatican.va/content/john-paul-ii/en/apost_exhortations/documents/hf_jp-ii_exh_25031992_pastores-dabo-vobis.html.
Kramer, Kenneth Paul, and Mechthild Gawlick. *Martin Buber's I and Thou: Practicing Living Dialogue.* New York: Paulist, 2003.
Kierkegaard, Søren. *Works of Love.* Translated by Howard Vincent Hong and Edna Hatlestad Hong. New York: HarperPerennial, 2009.
Lane, Thomas J. *The Catholic Priesthood: Biblical Foundations.* Steubenville: Emmaus Road, 2016.
Long, Thomas G., and Leonora Tubbs Tisdale, eds. *Teaching Preaching as a Christian Practice: A New Approach to Homiletical Pedagogy.* Louisville: Westminster John Knox, 2008.
Lichtenwalner, Andrew W. "The Church as the Bride of Christ in Magisterial Teaching from Leo XIII to John Paul II." PhD diss., Catholic University of America, 2012.
Luker, Kristin. *Salsa Dancing into the Social Sciences: Research in an Age of Info-glut.* Boston: Harvard University Press, 2008.
Mahohoma, Takesure. "Difficult Texts: *Koinonia*, Acts 2.42." *Theology* 120.5 (2017) 364–66. doi:10.1177/0040571X17710202.
Malmström, Hans. "Engaging the Congregation: The Place of Metadiscourse in Contemporary Preaching." *Applied Linguistics* 37.4 (August 2016) 561–82. https://doi.org/10.1093/applin/amu052.
MacDonald, Margaret Y. *Colossians and Ephesians.* Sacra Pagina Series 17. Collegeville: Liturgical, 2008.

McClure, John S. *Preaching Words: 144 Key Terms in Homiletics.* Louisville: Westminster John Knox, 2007.

McGovern, Thomas. *Priestly Celibacy Today.* Princeton, NJ: Scepter, 1998.

———. *Priestly Identity: A Study in the Theology of Priesthood.* Dublin: Four Courts, 2000.

Office for the Liturgical Celebrations of the Supreme Pontiff. "The Priest and the Paschal Triduum." http://www.vatican.va/news_services/liturgy/details/ns_lit_doc_20100412_sac-triduo_en.html.

Ouellet, Marc. *Mystery and Sacrament of Love: A Theology of Marriage and the Family for the New Evangelization.* Translated by Michelle K. Borras and Adrian J. Walker. Grand Rapids: Eerdmans, 2015.

Order for Celebrating Matrimony. 3rd Typical Edition. Washington, DC: USCCB, 2016.

Paul VI, Pope. *Humanae Vitae.* http://www.vatican.va/content/paul-vi/en/encyclicals/documents/hf_p-vi_enc_25071968_humanae-vitae.html.

Payne, Philip. "What about Headship? From Hierarchy to Equality." In *Mutual by Design: A Better Model of Christian Marriage*, edited by Elizabeth Beyer, 141–61. Minneapolis: CBE International, 2017.

Pesarchick, Robert A. *The Trinitarian Foundation of Human Sexuality as Revealed by Christ According to Hans Urs von Balthasar: The Revelatory Significance of the Male Christ and the Male Ministerial Priesthood.* Roma: Ed. Pontificia University Gregoriana, 2000.

Philbert, Paul J. *The Priesthood of the Faithful: Key to a Living Church.* Collegeville: Liturgical, 2005.

Pilon, Mark A. "Pastors and Stability of Office." *Homiletic and Pastoral Review*, March 25, 2009. https://www.hprweb.com/2009/03/pastors-and-stability-of-office/.

Pitre, Brant J. *Jesus the Bridegroom: The Greatest Love Story Ever Told.* New York: Image, 2014.

Polaski, Sandra H. *A Feminist Introduction to Paul.* St. Louis: Chalice, 2005.

Power, Dermot. *A Spiritual Theology of the Priesthood: The Mystery of Christ and the Mission of the Priest.* Washington, DC: The Catholic University of America Press, 1998.

Preaching the Mystery of Faith: The Sunday Homily. Washington, DC: USCCB, 2013.

Ratzinger, Joseph. *Dogma and Preaching: Applying Christian Doctrine to Daily Life.* Edited by Michael J. Miller. Translated by Matthew J. O'Connell. San Francisco: Ignatius, 2011.

Reid, Robert S., ed. *Slow of Speech and Unclean Lips: Contemporary Images of Preaching Identity.* Eugene, OR: Cascade, 2010.

Rice, Charles. "Authority of the Preacher." In *The New Interpreter's Handbook of Preaching*, edited by Paul Scott Wilson, 219–23. Nashville: Abingdon, 2008.

Rites of Ordination of a Bishop, of Priests, and of Deacons. 2nd Typical Edition. Washington, DC: USCCB, 2003.

Roberts, Benjamin A. "From Benedict to Francis: A Brief Survey of Papal Teaching on Preaching, 1917–2013." *Homiletic and Pastoral Review*, December 20, 2016. https://www.hprweb.com/2016/12/from-benedict-to-francis/.

Roberts, Sam. "Majority of Marriages End Before 25 Years, Census Finds." *New York Times*, September 19, 2007. http://www.nytimes.com/2007/09/19/us/19cnd-census.html.

Rubio, Julie Hanlon. *A Christian Theology of Marriage and Family*. New York: Paulist, 2003.
Schneiders, Sandra M. *The Revelatory Text: Interpreting the New Testament as Sacred Scripture*. Collegeville: Liturgical, 1999.
Schwartz, Robert M. *Servant Leaders of the People of God: An Ecclesial Spirituality for American Priests*. New York: Paulist, 1989.
Scola, Angelo. *The Nuptial Mystery*. Ressourcement: Retrieval & Renewal in Catholic Thought. Translated by Michelle K. Borras. Grand Rapids: Eerdmans, 2005.
Selin, Gary. *Priestly Celibacy: Theological Foundations*. Washington, DC: Catholic University of America Press, 2016.
Sensing, Tim. *Qualitative Research: A Multi-Methods Approach to Projects for Doctor of Ministry Theses*. Eugene, OR: Wipf & Stock, 2011.
Smith, Sarah J. "Reader/Listener Response." In *The New Interpreter's Handbook of Preaching*, edited by Paul Scott Wilson, 161–63. Nashville: Abingdon, 2008.
Speyr, Adrianne von. *The World of Prayer*. Translated by Graham Harrison. San Francisco: Ignatius, 1985.
Tait, Mark. *Jesus, the Divine Bridegroom in Mark 2:18–22: Mark's Christology Upgraded*. Roma: Gregorian & Biblical, 2010.
The Liturgy of the Hours. Washington, DC: USCCB, 1981.
The Roman Missal. 3rd Typical Edition. Washington, DC: USCCB, 2011.
Tisdale, Leonora Tubbs. *Preaching as Local Theology and Folk Art*. Minneapolis: Fortress, 2010.
Thomas, Frank A. "From Problem through Gospel Assurance to Celebration." In *Patterns of Preaching*, edited by Ronald Allen, 43–48. St. Louis: Chalice, 2006.
Toups, David L. *Reclaiming Our Priestly Character*. Omaha: Institute for Priestly Formation, IPF, 2008.
Torrell, Jean Pierre. *A Priestly People: Baptismal Priesthood and Priestly Ministry*. Translated by Peter Heinegg. Mahwah: Paulist, 2013.
University of Michigan. "Seven-year Itch? Boredom Can Hurt A Marriage." *ScienceDaily*, April 29, 2009. www.sciencedaily.com/releases/2009/04/090429172241.htm.
Vatican Council II. *Lumen Gentium*. http://www.vatican.va/archive/hist_councils/ii_vatican_council/documents/vat-ii_const_19641121_lumen-gentium_en.html.
———. *Presbyterorum Ordinis*. http://www.vatican.va/archive/hist_councils/ii_vatican_council/documents/vat-ii_decree_19651207_presbyterorum-ordinis_en.html.
Wallace, James A., ed. *Preaching in the Sunday Assembly: A Pastoral Commentary on Fulfilled in Your Hearing; Commentary and Text*. Collegeville: Liturgical, 2010.
Wilson, Paul S., ed. *The New Interpreter's Handbook of Preaching*. Nashville: Abingdon, 2008.
Weigel, George. "Pastors Are Not Interchangeable Parts." *First Things*, June 2013. https://www.firstthings.com/web-exclusives/2013/06/pastors-are-not-interchangeable-parts.
Wood, Susan K. *Sacramental Orders*. Collegeville: Liturgical, 2000.

www.ingramcontent.com/pod-product-compliance
Lightning Source LLC
Chambersburg PA
CBHW070930160426
43193CB00011B/1642